MIND YOUR OWN BUSINESS

Economics at Work

David Jacobson
Terrence McDonough
Keith Warnock

Oak Tree Press

Dublin

in association with

Services, Industrial, Professional and Technical Union
(SIPTU)

Oak Tree Press
Merrion Building
Lower Merrion Street
Dublin 2, Ireland
http://www.oaktreepress.com

A catalogue record of this book is
available from the British Library.

ISBN 1 86076 209 3

Printed in the Republic of Ireland by Colour Books Ltd.

 *Supported by the ADAPT Community Initiative
of the European Social Fund*

Contents

Foreword

There was a time when being an employee meant that you really had to "mind your own business": ask no awkward questions, do what you were told, know your place and leave financial or business affairs to those who knew better. In that simple world of master and servant the less you knew about economic performance or financial management the better. Your financial responsibility extended no further than your pay packet and you were expected to consider yourself lucky to have one.

But now we live in a very different world. Every day we sell our intelligence, our skill, our insights, our knowledge and our imagination. Our ability to anticipate and to resolve problems is considered essential to the good health of our enterprise. We are expected to understand the business environment within which we operate and to conduct ourselves accordingly. We now share the responsibility, the management and hopefully the rewards of business success. Even if we don't have a financial investment in the enterprise, we invest our talents and our time to improve the quality of the goods or services produced. We have a more intimate personal relationship with our business than any financial shareholder.

Understandably, owners, managers and shareholders have always concerned themselves with the economic vitality and profitability of their own enterprise. They have always recognised that their immediate and long-term economic interests are bound up with the business success. This has often led to an exclusiveness and elitism which determined the nature of rewards systems. Share options, profit-related income, annual performance bonuses or gain-sharing were exclusively available for executive management — while pay and salary were the only options available for employees. It is becoming increasingly evident that such a demarcation between different categories of employees serves as an obstacle to good enterprise management and fails to address the realities of the modern enterprise.

In recent years, we in SIPTU have sought to challenge that two-tier approach which rewards management differently than it rewards other categories of employees. We favour a multi-stakeholder view of the enterprise, which acknowledges that many groups and categories contribute to the success or failure of an enterprise and each group must have their contribution acknowledged. We believe that wages should be supplemented by a share of the profits, either through a share offer scheme, a gain-sharing scheme or a profit-related bonus scheme. We do not envisage employees depending on such schemes for their basic remuneration but we believe that such schemes provide a useful added value mechanism for rewarding extra effort and commitment to the goals of the enterprise.

SIPTU has long held the view that in determining an appropriate wages policy for the trade union movement, both distributional and economic development objectives come into play. For the objective is not only to secure rising living standards for those already at work; it is also to ensure growing employment opportunities for those not yet at work. By definition, therefore, the trade union movement is concerned with pursuing wages policy in the context of an overall growth strategy to ensure both rising consumption and rising investment.

In October 1999 the Economic and Social Research Institute published its *Medium-Term Review 1999–2005*. In the course of its evaluation of the past 20 years, the ESRI observed that in order to generate the major increase in employment that finally materialised in the 1990s, Ireland's competitiveness needed to improve dramatically through a steady rise in the profits share of output but that this had now gone far enough and that labour's share should now rise over the first decade and a half of the new millennium. But no less important is the added impetus now given in the *Programme for Prosperity and Fairness* to supplement wage increases with encouraging increased participation in the profits component as well.

The research paper on *Profit-Sharing, Employee Share Ownership and Gain-sharing*, which was published by the National Economic and Social Council in May 2000, made a significant contribution to current thinking in this area. It points out that one of the potential benefits of profit-sharing is its ability to contribute to stabilising the economy at a high level of employment — that profit-sharing can in fact contribute to the achievement and maintenance of full employment itself. This in turn is an argument for providing tax relief for profit-sharing. But the NESC Research Paper also goes on to conclude that the productivity benefits associated with profit-sharing and other group incentives are stronger when such incentives are combined with other forms of employee involvement. Moreover, the NESC also cites substantial evidence that the beneficial effects of new work practices are stronger when these practices are used both in combination with each other and with support from other human resource practices, such as training and appropriate compensation policies.

In short, the concept behind *Mind Your Own Business* is rapidly achieving greater comprehensiveness and depth.

No less significant is the renewed impetus to such developments which is coming in the shape of policy initiatives at European Union level. In June 2000, the European Commission published its communication on *The New Social Policy Agenda*. Among the Commission's declared objectives were the development of a positive and proactive approach to change by promoting adequate information for both companies and employees, and addressing the employment and social consequences of economic and market integration, such as mergers, acquisitions, etc. The Commission holds that this will require strong action by social partners at all levels (European, national, sectoral and company), and the development of shared responsibility between business and employees. It states that the action required at European level on these issues includes the final adoption of pending legalisation proposals, notably the worker participation provisions of the European Company Statute and the Directive establishing a general framework for informing and consulting employees in the European Community. But no less significant is the Commission proposal that in 2001 it should launch a communication and action plan on the financial participation of workers.

SIPTU also wishes to promote a far greater degree of openness and transparency in economic life, enabling employees to understand the business they are in. To make that meaningful, we want to increase the level of basic economic literacy among people at work and improve their ability to know their own business. That is equally important with payment systems, pension arrangements, investment decisions and performance measurement.

With this book, *Mind Your Own Business*, SIPTU is hoping to increase the understanding of company-related economic and accountancy data. We hope the approach of using cartoons, questions and answers, quotations, etc. will facilitate learning and provide worthwhile insights into commonly used economic, accountancy and business terms. We are not seeking to make economists of those who use this text but we are hoping that it will dispel some of the mystery that often surrounds economic debate. Just as our parents had to learn the harsh economic reality of the family budgets, the cost of living, the price of food, heating and clothing, the importance of savings, rewards and the consequences of indebtedness, we now must learn to understand the new economic factors that will determine our living standards.

This is an important book for all these reasons.

Des Geraghty,
General President,
Services, Industrial, Professional and
Technical Union (SIPTU).

Acknowledgements

The impetus for SIPTU's Adapt project and this book was provided by the General Officers and National Executive Council of the Services, Industrial, Professional, and Technical Union (SIPTU). They have extended every facility and encouragement throughout the development of both the project and this book. The SIPTU Adapt project was led by Des Geraghty, SIPTU's General President, who supported and encouraged both the project and the development of this book.

The aim of SIPTU's Adapt project was to develop criteria and models of enterprise industrial relations following a bottom-up approach that would be sustainable in an environment of continuous change and competition.

The authors of the book are Professor David Jacobson, Dublin City University, Dr. Terrence McDonough, National University of Ireland and Dr Keith Warnock, National University of Ireland. Both Professor Jacobson and Dr McDonough worked closely with SIPTU's Education and Training Department in developing and delivering SIPTU's Adapt project.

This book would not have been possible without the involvement and support of the SIPTU shop stewards, activist members, officials and management of the ten participating enterprises in the project. This book is based on their experiences and participation in the project's national and enterprise-based training courses, workshops and seminars.

The support and assistance afforded by other contributors to the text and presentation of the book is also acknowledged.

These include Manus O'Riordan, Head of SIPTU's Research Department, Rosheen Callender, SIPTU's National Equality Officer, Maureen Maloney, and also to Pat Coughlan, Francis Devine, John McCartney, and Martin Naughton of SIPTU College.

The union also acknowledges with thanks the assistance of Léargas and the European Union Adapt Human Resources Community Initiative.

Ron Kelly
SIPTU Adapt Project Manager
February 2001

The authors wish to thank Marian Brady, Gabrielle Warnock and Dr Sarah Ingle for invaluable advice on the text. We are most grateful to Maureen Maloney, the author of "New Forms of Compensation" in Section Three. Thanks also to Richard Chapman and to Carol Simpson for permission to use their cartoons.

About the Authors

Professor David Jacobson teaches economics and political economy at Dublin City University Business School. He has worked closely with SIPTU, evaluating programmes aimed at improving partnership approaches to running and developing firms in Ireland. His previous books include a study of public enterprise in Ireland and a textbook on Industrial Economics. He also co-edited the 1998 publication, *In the Shadow of the Tiger: New Approaches to Combating Social Exclusion*.

Dr Terrence McDonough is a lecturer in economics at National University of Ireland, Galway, and a member of SIPTU. He has extensive experience in labour education in both the United States and Ireland.

Keith Warnock graduated with a law degree from Dublin University, and subsequently qualified as a chartered accountant, working in England and the USA. After studying for a postgraduate degree in the University of Manchester, he returned to Ireland and has lectured in accounting at the National University of Ireland, Galway, since 1977. He has been Editor of the *Irish Accounting Review* since 1994, has published articles in academic and professional journals, and is a regular contributor of poetry to the journal *Critical Perspectives on Accounting*.

How to Use this Book

This is not a typical business text. There are many texts published discussing economics, accounting and management. This book differs in taking up these subjects from the point of view of working people. Standard texts often make these subjects seem mysterious and difficult. Even worse, an approach is often taken which sets up working people as the problem to be solved. Sound economics is said to be about holding down labour costs. Management is about forcing employees to work harder. We believe these approaches ignore the fact that working people are the ones who *produce* the economy. Our efforts are what make it happen. Working people are also the major contributors to the success of individual enterprises.

Because of our experience, knowledge and skills at the centre of the economy and the enterprise, working people are the economy's greatest untapped resource. Unions have recognised this important fact and have begun to demand a greater role for workers and their organisations in business and government decision-making. Worker participation makes good economic sense, but more than this, basic democratic principles demand we have a strong voice in the big decisions which intimately affect our lives. This depends on the active participation of every union member.

This book is written to provide Irish union members with some of the knowledge and skills we need to deepen our participation in business and the economy at national, international, and local level. Changes in business and the economy have also meant that workers and trade unions face new challenges. The new international economy and new business strategies do not lessen the need for employees to have strong and vigilant trade union representation. The successful pursuit of workers' interests demands a better and more detailed understanding of economics, accounting and management.

The first section of this book takes up the basics of the economy as it relates to working people. It discusses the so-called Celtic Tiger, the global economy, the origin of profits, and the role of the state. Economics is about the basic rules and structure of the game. The second section takes up how to keep score. It covers the basics of accounting. The third section is about strategy. It takes a close look at the differing strategies that management uses in its pursuit of profits.

You don't have to read the book straight through. Though the economics section provides some basic background understanding, each section can stand on its own. For instance, you don't have to read Section Two before reading Section Three. We have tried to make the book as accessible as possible. But accessible is not the same as simplified. When you have completed each section, we hope you will have a basic but sophisticated understanding of economics, accounting, and management from the worker's point of view.

SECTION ONE

ECONOMICS: LEARNING THE BASICS OF THE GAME

Most business education starts with an introductory course in economics. It is important to understand the national economy within which a business must operate. In order to make intelligent decisions, players in the business world must know what's been happening in the overall economy and why. For instance:

- They must be able to speculate about which current trends have staying power and which don't.

- They have to understand the impact of the state of the economy on the markets for capital, raw material and labour.

- They must have a sense of where the general economy is driving the demand for their products.

- They have to anticipate the actions of economic policy-makers and other players in the economy.

These days, it is also essential to know about the international economy. Globalisation is now the background environment in which nearly all businesses must survive. Decision-makers must know the role their country and their industry plays in the international markets. They need to know where foreign competition is likely to come from. They need to understand developments in the foreign economies that are driving international growth or recession. They have to anticipate the movements of international finance.

But more than all these things, a proper understanding of economic theory is needed to understand the basics of the economic game. If you've missed a deep understanding of the underlying structure of the game, all your training and playing strategy is likely to come to nothing. An ability to tally the score without understanding the basic play would only make a player look ridiculous.

In Section One, we will not take up all these economic topics in detail, but we will provide a basic introduction. Chapter 1 looks at the Celtic Tiger and its impact on the Irish economy and the well-being of Irish working people. Chapter 2 argues that, in a capitalist economy, profits are the most important factor to understand. Unlike most economics texts, however, this chapter will develop an **understanding of profits from the working person's perspective**. Chapter 3 will examine the role of government in determining the distribution of income in society.

Chapter 1

Ireland: The Lady or the Tiger?

In this chapter:

❖ **Is the Celtic Tiger real?**

❖ **Is the Celtic Tiger all he's cracked up to be?**

❖ **How has the Tiger affected Irish working people?**

❖ **How does Ireland fit in the global economy?**

Suddenly it's fashionable to be Irish. Irish pubs are springing up all over Europe and in some of the most unlikely places from Shanghai to Kathmandu. The hospitality industry in America and Europe is clamouring for young, educated, hardworking and friendly Irish staff. All over the world people are talking about Ireland, Irish music and dance, and our thriving young computer industry.

Historically, Ireland was pictured as a woman. Prior to the twentieth century, she was often painted or sketched as a maiden holding a harp — a symbol, no doubt, of our Celtic cultural past. After independence, she became Kathleen Ní Houlihan or Queen Maeve as portrayed on the old £1 note. More recently, however, instead of the lady, there's been a tiger behind every door.

First, there was the *Emerald Tiger*, to distinguish him from the Asian tiger economies. Now he's fully grown and confidently called the *Celtic Tiger*, though he's still often striped green instead of the traditional tiger orange. Even people who first resisted this description of the Irish economy have given in and accepted it, though many prefer to think of the tiger as a mother with cubs, all of whom must be cared for.

So what's behind this astonishing transformation?

THE ROARING TIGER

The most startling evidence for the emergence of the tiger is the big rise in the Irish GDP. The GDP, the *Gross Domestic Product*, is the standard measure of the output of the economy. Changes in the GDP are the most important indicators of growth. Since the tiger started, real Irish GDP has more than doubled. This rate of GDP growth is unprecedented.

The chart below looks at the years from 1987 to 2000. It gives the percentage growth rate for the United States, the EU and Ireland. You can see that in each year Irish GDP growth outstrips that of America and Europe as a whole.

Figure 1: Growth Rates Compared

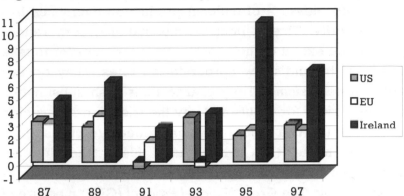

Source: OECD

THE EXPERTS RIDE THE TIGER

One of the most amazing things about the tiger is that no one predicted him! All of the economic experts thought that major changes were needed or the Irish lady would be riding a Celtic donkey into the foreseeable future. In fact, many economists are still sceptical about the tiger and argue that he's not all he's cracked up to be.

Below are some of the arguments put forward by various economists about the so-called tiger economy.

The Paper Tiger

Some economists have pointed out that the Gross Domestic Product (GDP) measure of national production overstates Ireland's prosperity. This is because multinational corporations exaggerate the extent of their Irish production in order to take advantage of Ireland's low corporate tax rates. They do this through *transfer pricing*. They charge their Irish subsidiaries low internal prices for inputs and pay the Irish operations high prices for output. As a result, the money measure of Irish production looks higher than it really is. If this is taken into account, the Irish economy is not doing as well as the GDP measure makes it look. The *Gross National Product* (GNP) measure of output can be used to correct for transfer pricing because it subtracts out multinational profits sent out of the country. Figure 2 shows the difference between Ireland's GDP and GNP performance. GNP is below GDP and the difference in the height of the two lines shows the gap.

Figure 2: The Difference between Ireland's GDP and GNP Performance

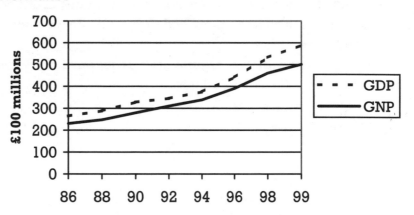

Source: Central Statistics Office

Though the GNP is definitely lower than the GDP, Ireland's output has still expanded substantially in recent years.

At the same time, neither GDP nor GNP take into account such increasing negatives as:

- The decline in leisure and family time
- Increasing congestion and travel time in our cities
- Environmental degradation.

A thorough examination of these kinds of factors could call into question whether we are really better off. (See the section on environmental accounting in Chapter 10.)

The Wind-up Tiger

Other economists have contended that Ireland's recent economic performance is due to a one-off injection of labour into the economy. This injection comes from:

- An increase in school leavers
- Returned emigrants
- The entry of more Irish women into the labour force.

The extra labour has wound up the Tiger and set off a period of unusual activity. But unlike the "Duracell Bunny" of the ads, the tiger cannot go on and on. Once the extra labour is absorbed, Ireland will return to normal rates of growth. The tiger will have wound down. Developing shortages like those in housing, childcare and transportation infrastructure will cause the tiger to wind down even faster.

The Celtic Tigger

Still other economists have pointed out that, like Tigger, the Winnie the Pooh character, the Celtic Tiger is not very fierce. Far from being king of the jungle, the impact of the tiger on the whole of the Irish economy has been limited. The tiger has relied on multinational investment. In Ireland, unlike in their home countries, multinational companies have only weak forward and backward linkages. This means they source relatively few inputs from Irish firms and have relatively few Irish customers, selling most of their production overseas. As a result, multinational investment has not stimulated enough growth in the indigenous Irish economy.

The Hobbesian Tiger

Other economists have argued that, like Hobbes in the *Calvin and Hobbes* cartoon, the tiger is a bit of an illusion, especially for the less well off. Under the tiger, inequality has risen and poverty rates have even gone up. The following table shows poverty rates (those receiving below 50 and 60 per cent of the average industrial wage) between 1987 and 1998. The first set of figures gives households below the poverty line. The second set gives persons below the line. The third set is especially worrying because it gives the percentage of children below the poverty line. The last set looks at female-headed households and is one measure of women's poverty.

Table 1: Relative Income Poverty Lines, 1987 and 1998

	1987	1994	1997	1998
Percentage of households below the line:				
50 per cent line	16.3	18.8	21.9	24.6
60 per cent line	28.5	34.6	36.5	33.4
Percentage of persons below the line:				
50 per cent line	18.9	20.7	21.7	20.5
60 per cent line	29.8	34.0	35.3	30.0
Percentage of children below the line:				
50 per cent line	25.5	29.3	23.7	N/A
60 per cent line	37.8	40.3	37.7	N/A
Percentage of female-headed households:				
50 per cent line	8.9	24.0	N/A	N/A
60 per cent line	30.8	52.7	N/A	N/A

Source: ESRI/Combat Poverty Agency; Callan et al. (1996), *Poverty in the 1990s*, Dublin: Oak Tree Press/ESRI.

These same commentators often point out that Ireland has been lucky to receive as much high tech multinational investment as it has. But because of the footloose character of international capital, these firms can withdraw almost as fast as they arrived. Because of this kind of insecurity, and the rising poverty and inequality, these economists argue the life of the tiger is likely to be (as seventeenth-century philosopher Thomas Hobbes said about life in the state of nature) nasty, brutish and short.

All in all, the Celtic Tiger has made a considerable contribution to Ireland's economic health, at least as it has been conventionally measured. Yet, the warnings of the sceptics must be taken seriously:

❖ The usual GDP measure overstates Ireland's prosperity.

❖ Multinational investment has not been extensively integrated into the local economy.

❖ High rates of growth cannot continue forever.

❖ Poverty, inequality and long-term unemployment remain significant social and economic problems.

IT'S A JUNGLE OUT THERE: IRELAND AND THE GLOBAL ECONOMY

Because of our geographic location and our history, Ireland has in the past been largely dependent on the British economy. This has changed substantially in recent years and we are now becoming increasingly integrated into the global economy. A large proportion of our investment comes from corporations which are based overseas. The majority of what we produce is shipped overseas. Much of what we consume is made or grown elsewhere. Irish performance is increasingly judged by international standards. More and more decisions are taken in light of global economic considerations.

Irish exports as a percentage of GDP have risen substantially since 1970. Figure 3 shows the percentage exported in 1970, 1980, and from 1987 to 2000.

Figure 3: Export of Goods as a Percentage of GDP, 1970–2000

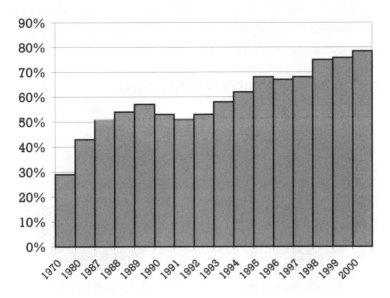

Source: Central Statistics Office; ESRI

This increase in exports has been accompanied by a substantial decline in Ireland's dependence on the British market and an increasing penetration of the markets of the rest of the world. The pie charts below show how Irish exports were divided between different destinations in 1960 and how this had changed by 2000.

Figure 4: Export Destinations

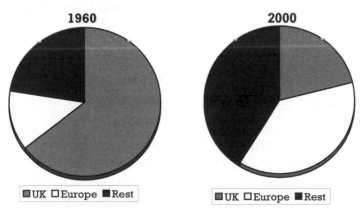

1960   2000

UK Europe Rest   UK Europe Rest

Transnationals make up an increasing share of both Irish GDP and Irish exports. This is reflected in the increasing share of foreign-owned industry in the manufacturing sector. The charts show the increase from 1987 to 1998.

Figure 5: Shares of Manufacturing Output

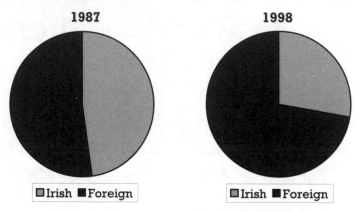

Table 2: Top Ten Foreign Multinationals in Ireland

1. Dell	Personal computer mfg and sales
2. Intel Ireland	Computer manufacturer
3. Microsoft	Software mfg/distribution
4. Oracle	Software mfg/sales
5. 3Com	PC adaptor card mfg
6. EMC BV	Computer data storage
7. Tesco	Supermarket retail
8. Janssen	Pharmaceuticals
9. Elan	Pharmaceuticals/health care
10. Swords Laboratories	Pharmaceuticals

Source: Business and Finance, February 2000.

Increasingly, economic policy is discussed in terms of international competitiveness. The competitiveness of a company is at base its ability to make profits in an international context. The next section will take a close look at where profits come from.

Chapter 2

Profits and Where They Come From

In this chapter:

❖ **Where do profits come from?**

❖ **What strategies do corporations pursue to increase profits in the workplace and in the marketplace?**

❖ **Which of these profit-making strategies produce conflict with the workforce and which offer the potential for participation?**

❖ **What is the impact of multinationalisation on these kinds of issues?**

❖ **Why do workers need trade union representation, even in the context of areas of participation?**

Traditional approaches to collective bargaining demanded that trade unions concern themselves with wages, benefits and working conditions. **Profits were the proper concern of management.** Today, unions are bidding to take a broader role in the life of the corporation. An essential element in this new approach is a concern about profits as well as other issues. This is true for a number of reasons:

- Effective participation depends on effective information. Much of the most important information concerns the company's performance. This information is contained in the company's accounts. These accounts keep track of the company's profitability. (We'll talk much more about accounts in the next section.)

- Issues like wages and working conditions are intimately linked to profits in complex ways, which we will discuss below.

- When companies talk about "competitiveness", they are really talking about the ability to make profits in an international context.

- Last but not least, profits are the main motivators in a capitalist system. They are the major touchstone in reference to which decisions are taken.

> **Key Point: Economic literacy is increasingly important to effective participation in union activity.**

THE BOTTOM LINE

In a capitalist economy, profits are the yardstick against which all decisions are measured. All economies must answer these basic questions:

1. **What is to be produced?**
2. **How are these things to be produced?**
3. **How is the production divided up? Who gets what?**

These questions have been answered in different ways in different times and places. In the capitalist economies of today, profits are the key factor in answering each of these questions.

> **Key Point: In a capitalist economy, profits motivate most of the key economic decisions.**

What Is to Be Produced?

Only those things that generate a profit will be produced. If beans make a profit, productive resources will move into beans. If yachts are the most profitable products, the economy will pull out all the stops to make yachts. If there is no profit to be made in low income housing, the private economy will not produce low income housing. During the Great Depression years, there were idle shoe factories, unemployed shoemakers, and millions who needed shoes. And yet no shoes were made. Why? Because there was no profit in it.

How Are Things Produced?

The most profitable method will be employed. Sometimes the most profitable method is the same as the most efficient method. But not always. Canning factories in California frequently alternated Spanish-speaking workers and English-speaking workers on their production lines. This prevented workers from communicating and organising. This kept wages low and profits high. But was it efficient? A more economically and socially desirable response would be to provide language training and other aids to integration, but that might not be profitable.

Who Gets What?

Profits determine the level of income for those who own property. The amount of profits paid out strongly influences how much is left over for the payment of wages.

A THEORY OF PROFITS

The first question we need to answer about profits is where they come from. Once we know where they come from we can then examine how they are measured. We do this in Section Two.

We can explain profits by first looking at the total amount of production in the economy. Imagine all the goods and services produced in the economy over the course of a year collected in one large box. This is called the *total product*.

Total
Product

The total product can then be divided into two basic categories. Since producing goods and services uses up raw materials and wears out machinery, some of the year's production must consist of replacement stocks of raw materials and replacement machinery. These products are collectively labelled *depreciation*. After the depreciation is separated out, what's left is called the *net product*.

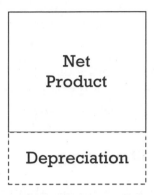

In turn, the net product is itself divided into two categories.

- The first category consists of *wage goods*. Wage goods can include food, clothing, housing, transportation, entertainment, anything that is purchased by working people with their wages. The wage goods make up the standard of living of the working population.

- After the wage goods are accounted for what is left over is the *surplus product*. It is this surplus product which becomes available for the payment of profits.

Since the contribution of the raw materials and machinery to the total product is accounted for by depreciation, both the wage goods and the goods whose sale generates profits are produced by the application of labour over the course of the year.

Thus profits consist of that portion of the labour expended by working people which *does not* come back to them in the form of wage goods. For this reason, this explanation of profits is called a *labour theory of profit*.

> **Key Point: Profits originate in the unpaid labour of working people.**

PROFITS IN DEPTH: DIVIDING UP THE SURPLUS PRODUCT

It is not just the owners of manufacturing companies who have a claim on the surplus product.

- Banks or financial capitalists take part of the surplus product in the form of interest

- Stores and other retail capitalists take part of the surplus in the form of retail profits

- Managers take part of the surplus product in the form of salaries

- The state takes part of the surplus product in the form of taxes.

This means that a firm's profits can be increased by minimising interest payments, "cutting out the middle man" in the form of the retailer, saving on management salaries and paying less tax. Many of these topics will turn up again in Section Two on accounts.

HOW DO CORPORATIONS PURSUE PROFITS?

This next section will examine the strategies pursued by corporations in search of increased profits.

Consider the picture we drew on page 17 of the labour theory of profits. Instead of representing the production of an entire economy, let the boxes represent the production of an individual company. We'll now look at the different ways in which the company could attempt to raise the profit share.

Corporations can seek to increase profits in two locations:

- **Within the workplace**

- **Within the marketplace.**

We will first consider strategies that can be pursued within the firm itself.

Increasing Profits in the Workplace

One possible strategy is through **lowering wages**. This can be achieved in different ways, for instance:

- Announcing or negotiating an hourly cut in wages

- Cutting back on workers' benefits

- Bringing in temporary workers outside the contract

- Hiring part-timers without benefits.

This kind of change is illustrated below.

 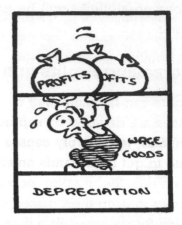

Still another strategy is through *increasing production*. This potentially increases the size of the surplus box.

Increased production can be achieved in two ways:

- Adopting more efficient production techniques — "working smarter". This could include training, new technology, improved working methods, changes in the work environment, and family friendly policies.

- Increasing the intensity of work — "working harder".

Both of these possibilities will be examined in more detail in Section 3.

These possibilities will be examined in more detail in Section Three.

Increasing Profits in the Marketplace

Profits can be increased in the marketplace by *raising prices*. Prices are decided by supply and demand. For a given level of demand, low supply causes prices to rise as consumers compete to get their hands on scarce goods. When supply is high, however, the market becomes flooded and producers are forced to drop their prices to offload the goods. A similar logic holds for demand. At a given level of supply, low demand implies less competition for goods, and producers must drop prices to attract buyers. When demand is high, however, there is competition for goods and services, and therefore they can be sold for higher prices.

General increases in the price level are called inflation and do not generally raise profits. A corporation's profits can be increased by raising prices in the absence of a general price increase. A specific corporation can charge higher prices if:

- It offers higher quality than its competitors, or

- It innovates and offers products or services its competitors can't.

Profits can also be increased at the other end of the production process by sourcing *cheaper inputs*.

Finally, profits can be raised by *increasing sales*. This can be accomplished through better marketing, or offering a better price if the increased sales justify the lower price per sale.

> *Key Point: Corporations can pursue a number of different strategies in seeking to improve profits.*

THE WAYS TO INCREASE PROFITS

We can now make a list of the basic strategies used to increase profits.

Strategies in the Marketplace:

1. *Raise quality*

2. *Innovate*

3. *Source cheaper inputs*

4. *Increase sales*

Strategies in the Workplace:

5. *Reduce wages*

6. *Increase effort*

7. *Increase efficiency*

AREAS OF CONFLICT AND AREAS OF PARTICIPATION

A look down this list of ways to increase profits reveals that some strategies hold the potential for conflict whereas others might be less contentious.

Conflictual strategies include *cutting wages* and *increasing effort without compensation*. It is important to remember that increasing effort without compensation is just as objectionable as cutting wages. The other strategies contain the potential for participation but may also be a source of conflict.

- More efficient techniques may be neutral to or actually improve working life, but some may also have the potential to contribute to deteriorating quality of work life.

- Producing a higher quality product is a positive goal, but not if it increases the intensity of work without compensation.

- Product innovation may protect high wage jobs, but pressures to innovate have created a high stress workplace in some companies.

- Sourcing cheaper inputs may improve a company's competitiveness, but employees cannot be expected to be enthusiastic if this involves outsourcing work to non-union plants.

- Increasing sales makes jobs more secure, but increased value for the consumer should not be bought at the cost of increasing conflict at work.

All of these points emphasise that while participation as well as conflict can play a role in labour relations, the potential for participation does not lessen the need for employees to have strong and vigilant trade union representation.

> **Key Point: Even within areas of participation, workers still retain distinct interests.´**

If workers' participation succeeds in raising revenue for the company, this can be paid out in either higher profits or higher wages. Participation does not mean traditional collective bargaining issues go away.

MULTINATIONAL CORPORATIONS AND THE ISSUE OF COMPETITIVENESS

Today, *competitiveness* is an issue both at the level of the individual corporation and at the level of the nation as a whole. All proposed changes in labour relations bring the question: will it increase or decrease competitiveness? National economic policy in many nations increasingly revolves around the issue of national competitiveness. Seldom do we hear a discussion of just what this competitiveness involves. **At base, being competitive is having the ability to make profits in an international context**.

We can examine the effect of participation in the international economy on the various strategies to raise profitability that were listed earlier. In this context, we can say who gains and who loses from multinationalisation.

WHO GAINS AND WHO LOSES?

Increasing Sales

Multinationalisation can potentially open up wider markets for company's products. This can increase profitability and make jobs more secure. In this area, multinationalisation is:

- An advantage to capital

- An advantage to workers.

Increasing Efficiency,
Raising Quality and
Innovating

In these three areas multinationalisation creates the opportunity for exposure to world class standards and competition. The multinational organisation is able to draw inspiration and ideas from many sources. In these areas, multinationalisation is:

- An advantage to capital

- A possible advantage for an active and educated workforce.

Sourcing Cheaper Inputs

Multinationalisation greatly expands the opportunity of the corporation to seek the cheapest inputs. To the extent that this involves finding the most efficient suppliers, everyone can benefit. This possibility, however, is probably outweighed by the tendency to seek supplies from low-wage countries and non-union plants. In this area, multinationalisation is:

- An advantage to capital

- A disadvantage to workers.

Increasing Effort

This issue is similar. Multinational corporations can seek the most docile labour forces in the different parts of the world. One plant can be played against another in demanding concessions on working conditions. In this area as well, multinationalisation is:

- An advantage to capital

- A disadvantage to workers.

Reducing Wages

Multinational corporations are in a position to seek the cheapest labour in various regions of the Third World and Eastern Europe. Corporations with multiple plants are able to play one segment of the workforce against another in demanding wage concessions. In the area of negotiating over wages, multinationalisation is an:

- Advantage to capital

- A disadvantage to workers.

Unsurprisingly, multinationalisation works to the advantage of capital. For the workforce the issue is more complex. It is necessary to draw up a balance sheet.

MULTINATIONALISATION: PROS AND CONS

Costs to Workers	Potential Benefits to Workers
Easier to cut wages	Increased efficiency, quality and innovation
Easier to force an increase in effort	Increased sales
Easier to outsource inputs	Only possible for an educated workforce

Multinationalisation poses many challenges for organised labour and opportunities only for an active and educated workforce. This underlines the importance of *continuing education* within the labour movement.

It is important to develop short- and medium-term strategies to deal with the global economy. In the long term, no one set of countries will have the monopoly on education and high skills. It is important to realise that ultimately the international economy will force all workers to either:

- **Compete harder**, or

- **Co-operate and develop international solidarity**.

UNEMPLOYMENT AND THE ROLE OF UNIONS

So far we have seen that the division of the net product between wage goods and surplus labour determines the distribution of income in society. We haven't yet discussed what determines where this division takes place — that is, how much goes to workers and how much goes to capital. Basically, the level of wages is determined by the relative bargaining power of workers and capital.

There are two basic factors that influence workers' bargaining power. The first factor is the level of unemployment. Unemployment affects workers' bargaining power directly. If the level of unemployment is low, firms cannot afford to lose employees. If few people are unemployed, leaving employees are very hard to replace. They have to be recruited away from their present employers. This means offering a more attractive package of wages, benefits and working conditions. Under these circumstances, when employees demand wage increases or improved conditions, the employer is forced to listen. It may be cheaper to grant worker demands rather than risk them leaving and having to recruit new employees.

On the other hand, if unemployment is high, workers will have little bargaining power. In response to requests for improvements, the employer can point to a long line of desperate jobseekers outside the personnel office. The employer will point out that there are plenty of people who would probably be willing to take the job at even less money. Workers seeking increases in pay may be happily shown the road. This means policies that promote full employment are important to workers, even those who are presently in secure employment.

The other major factor that influences workers' bargaining power is unionisation. The idea behind unions is that workers stop competing with each other for the available jobs. With a union, workers confront the employer in a united way.

Employers and individual workers cannot confront each other as equals. Individually, the worker has little power. The lone worker has nothing but his or her labour to sell. If the worker loses the job, their standard of living and that of their family hangs in the balance. If the employer loses one worker, he or she can usually hire another. Only when workers are organised into unions can this basic imbalance between employers and workers be at least partially redressed.

It is not surprising then that unionised workers are better paid than those without a union. Many studies have shown that there is a definite financial advantage to union membership. Even when factors like industry, training and age are strictly comparable, union members take home more money than non-union members. Of course, unions are not just about wages. Unions also bargain about the conditions of work. Unions protect the employee against arbitrary and unfair treatment. The union seeks to provide the workers with a voice in the workplace and at national level with government and employers. Organisation and solidarity provide dignity and respect.

Another important factor that is influenced by the level of unionisation is political power. All bargaining takes place within a framework of laws and state action. The experience of Thatcherism in Britain demonstrates that if workers lose influence in government, they can be seriously weakened in the workplace. The next chapter looks briefly at the role of the state in the economy.

DEBATE

Q. "Labour isn't the only input into the production process. If plant and machinery raise the productivity of labour, shouldn't the owners receive a return for their contribution to production? Aren't profits just a fair return for capital's contribution?"

A. "Of course machinery and equipment increase the amount of goods and services workers can produce. But these factors increase the productivity of *labour*. A hammer raises the productivity of a good joiner, but the hammer has no productivity in the absence of the joiner. How can you calculate how much of the output is due to the hammer and how much to the joiner? Even if the capital is productive, that doesn't mean the money should rightly go to the owner of the capital who could be oceans away from the actual production."

Q. "It's the owners of the capital who take the risks. You don't know the outcome when you start a business or invest more money in it. Profits have to exist in order to reward this kind of risk-taking."

A. "What is the owner risking? Losing his capital and having to go to work for a living? Working people face this condition every day, not just as a risk but as a certainty. Besides, workers take risks on the job every day which they are not compensated for."

Q. "The money to invest in a business has to be saved in the first place. Profits are just the reward for the sacrifice of saving."

A. "Most saving is done by the corporations themselves through retained earnings or by the wealthy. There's not much personal sacrifice in that."

Chapter 3

The Role of the State

In this chapter:

❖ **What is the importance of government to workers?**

❖ **How does the taxation system affect workers directly?**

❖ **Is government spending of greater benefit to employers or employees?**

❖ **How does the state involve itself directly in industrial relations?**

During and after World War II, the state came to play a bigger role in the life of the economy in all western countries. This was due to the expansion of military spending but was also due to the establishment of the welfare state. Expenditure on medical care, housing, education and social security all increased. This was generally the case in Ireland as well. Indeed, Irish spending per capita rose faster than the European average. The chart below traces the growth of state expenditure in Ireland as a proportion of GNP.

Figure 6: Central Government Expenditure as a Percentage of GNP

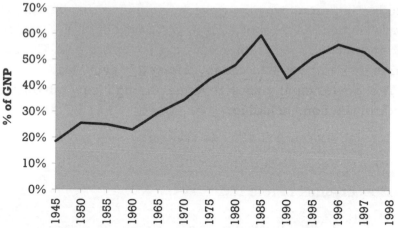

Source: Aidan Kane (1996), "Irish Fiscal Policy", PhD, Trinity College, Dublin.

THE STATE AND PRIVATE PROPERTY

Government plays a complicated, many-faceted role in influencing the distribution of income and determining the relative well-being of the different classes in society. At the most basic level, the state guarantees the right of employers to keep the profit generated in business. (Remember that profit is the surplus labour produced by the working population.) Profits can only exist if workers do not own any means of production and must work for others. The institution of private property means that the owners of the workplace, not the workers, are entitled to possession of whatever is produced in that workplace. This situation is created by the law and enforced by the state. By law, the workers must content themselves with their wages.

Of course, products don't become profits until they are sold. The state has a very important role in guaranteeing the existence of markets. The most basic way it does this is through the enforcement of contracts. If a buyer does not pay or a supplier fails to deliver on products paid for, the wronged party can sue through the courts. If the contract was valid, the government will enforce payment.

TAXATION

Another important way the government influences the distribution of income is through its powers of taxation. We all know our after-tax income is different from our gross pay. The same is true for everyone who cannot completely avoid tax.

The government raises revenue through several different kinds of taxation, including:

- Income tax or PAYE (Pay As You Earn)

- VAT or Value Added Tax

- Corporation or Profit Tax

- Capital gains tax

- Capital acquisitions tax

- DIRT tax (Deposit Interest Retention Tax).

The following table shows the share of government revenue from four basic kinds of tax.

Figure 7: Shares of Total Tax Take

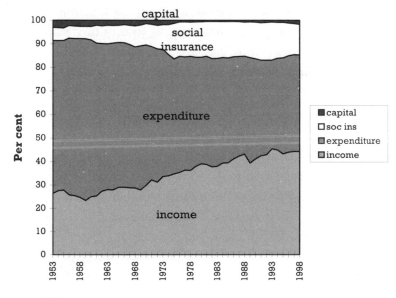

Source: CSO

Taxes paid by employers must come out of the surplus labour produced by employees. Taxes paid by workers which don't come back to them in the form of government-provided goods and services also come from the surplus labour of workers. So at the end of the day, it is the working population which provides the resources for government.

Nevertheless, different groups pay different taxes at different rates. Consequently, government tax policy can alter the distribution of income. Economists call the topic of who pays what percentage of which taxes the study of *tax incidence*. The arguments can get quite complicated and technical; nevertheless, some statements are safe to assume:

- Profit taxes and capital gains taxes generally reduce net profits though companies can partially recoup taxes by raising prices.

- VAT falls on everyone who consumes products.

Since lower income families are forced by necessity to spend a larger percentage of their incomes than higher income families, VAT falls disproportionately on lower incomes. Theoretically a graduated income tax with tax rates rising as incomes rise can fall more heavily on the high incomes. In reality there are many ways to shelter income from tax. In practice the PAYE worker pays a disproportionate share of taxation.

(IN MUCH THE SAME WAY AS IT'S EASIER TO SHEAR A SHEEP THAN A LION)

GOVERNMENT SPENDING

Still another way in which the government can alter the distribution of income in society is through its spending programmes. The basic question here is: do you get back more or less from the government than you paid in? Many government activities will benefit all citizens. Some, however, will primarily benefit workers and others will primarily benefit employers.

Government goods and services which raise the standard of living of working people are referred to by economists as the *social wage*. Examples of social wage programmes include:

- Public health care
- Unemployment benefits
- Community facilities.

Social security policies are especially important, because the availability of government support takes some of the sting out of the threat of unemployment. The level of unemployment payments also serve to put a floor under wages. At the very least, employers must pay better than the unemployment benefit.

Figure 8: Social Spending (1963–1998)

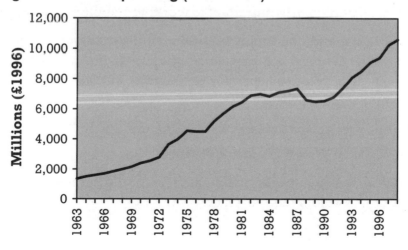

Source: CSO

Many government spending programmes are primarily intended to benefit employers. These may include:

- Subsidies for research and development

- Grants for locating in certain areas

- The provision of transport infrastructure — roads and bridges.

Whether public spending disproportionately benefits working people or business can substantially alter the distribution of income in society.

DIRECT INVOLVEMENT IN INDUSTRIAL RELATIONS

The government gets directly involved in industrial relations in a number of ways.

State Employees

One of the most obvious is that the government must establish a system of industrial relations and bargaining with its *own* employees. Bargaining between the government and state employees is particularly important to working people because:

1. The terms and conditions of public employment often serve to set a standard for private negotiations. If the state mistreats its employees, private employers will feel they have licence to do the same.

2. Public workplace issues often affect the quality of government services to working communities.

For these reasons, trade unions have seen the organisation of government employees as a high priority.

Labour Law

The government often passes laws that make it easier or harder for employees to form unions and bargain collectively. Sometimes the state actively moves to break unions and prevent worker organisation. This can be done through police or military interventions in strike situations and through the arrest and harassment of labour leaders. This kind of state activity took place in Thatcher's Britain and is common in many Third World countries.

Alternatively, states can encourage or even require employers to recognise unions and bargain collectively. State action can also be important for improving conditions at work. Health and safety legislation is a prominent example.

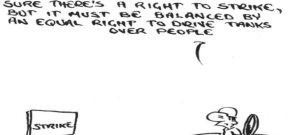

Minimum Wage Laws

The government can intervene in wage setting by establishing a minimum wage. A government-enforced minimum wage is important in protecting low-wage and unorganised workers from exploitation. Increases in the minimum wage tend to have

ripple effects up the wage scale and are consequently important even for workers making well above the minimum wage.

Employers and many economists have opposed minimum
wage legislation. They argue that setting a floor on wages will
prevent less productive, often young, entry-level workers from
finding work. There is little hard evidence to support this con-
tention, however. Recent studies in the US have been unable to
locate this effect.

Reducing Unemployment

The big role unemployment plays in determining the bargaining power of labour means that state economic policies are extremely important. It is essential that state policy should target
the elimination of unemployment as a primary goal. Traditionally, states used fiscal and monetary policy to target unemployment.

Fiscal policy involved increasing the overall demand for
goods and services by manipulating government spending
and/or taxes. In a small open economy like Ireland, these kinds
of measures are limited in effectiveness because much of the
additional demand goes towards increased imports and doesn't
create domestic jobs.

The other option the state had was monetary policy. An increase in the supply of money meant that banks had to compete
for borrowers. Interest rates were lowered. Lower interest rates
meant more investment and more demand and employment.
With the advent of European monetary union, monetary policy
is no longer set in Ireland but determined on a Europe-wide
basis.

This situation leaves the Irish state with three remaining options:

- The state can directly lower the level of unemployment by
  increasing the number of government employees. This kind
  of action can be particularly effective in employing the

long-term unemployed and taking up the slack in the labour market during recessions.

- The state can pursue an industrial policy aimed at encouraging domestic investment or attracting foreign multinationals.

- The third option the state can pursue is national wage and price agreements.

National Agreements

When the state promotes national agreements, economists refer to this as pursuing an *incomes policy*. These agreements are usually negotiated at national level. Employers are generally represented by business organisations like IBEC (Irish Business and Employers Confederation). Workers are represented by the labour federations like ICTU (Irish Congress of Trade Unions). The government will also attend the talks. In the last round of negotiations in Ireland representation was broadened to include social organisations such as those representing communities and the unemployed.

In order to get the parties to sign up to these agreements, both business and unions must believe they benefit in some way. From the point of view of business, national agreements create a stable climate of industrial relations. Employers know that disputes will be limited for the life of the agreement. They know roughly what their wage bills are going to be. This means that they can plan for the medium term.

If things go as hoped, this stability will encourage a higher level of investment than would otherwise be the case. This increased level of investment will contribute to creating higher levels of employment. For this reason, the promotion of national agreements, or incomes policies, is considered to be an unemployment-reducing programme.

If the agreements work as planned, working people benefit from the increased level of employment. As argued above, reducing unemployment is a prime goal of the labour movement. National agreements also have other advantages for unions. We established that many of the policies adopted by the state, like taxation, labour law and government spending have an important impact on the distribution of income. Bringing the government explicitly into the negotiations allows unions to directly influence these state policies.

National agreements also allow unions to engage in solidarity wage bargaining. Often the lowest paid workers have the least bargaining power. If each group of workers conducts separate negotiations, low paid workers will often be the least successful and income inequality will increase. National agreements mean that unions can bargain to raise the incomes of the least well off and consequently lower the level of income inequality. Greater equality among working people creates greater levels of solidarity and sets the stage for greater successes in the future.

Another advantage of national bargaining is that it puts the distribution of income on the national agenda. The bargaining itself becomes national news. This makes clear that setting wages is a complex social and political process. Business and many conservative economists often argue that the distribution of income is determined by impersonal market forces. If this is true, union organisation can have little impact and is a waste of resources. National agreements make it clear that income distribution is determined by the relative bargaining power of capital and labour. It becomes obvious that workers interests must be collectively represented.

National bargaining has the following advantages for unions:

- It can result in lower levels of unemployment.

- It can decrease inequality and promote solidarity among working people.

- It makes the need for worker organisation to bargain with capital and the state explicit.

"Our continued involvement in centralised national bargaining since 1987 was based on a determination by our trade union movement to shape a modern Ireland, which would be a better and fairer place for people to live, work and care for our communities and families. We wanted this generation to have access to well-paid and satisfying work. We wanted properly funded public services, access to housing, access to health care, education, pensions, sick pay, adequate social welfare and social insurance that caters for our future as well as our present needs. We want to create a successful social economy, not a selfish, rip-off, greedy, dog-eat-dog society propagated by Thatcher and her right-wing disciples in the UK, or by some home-grown Thatcherites." — Des Geraghty, SIPTU General President

Points to take away from Section One

- ❖ The Celtic Tiger has led to substantial growth in the Irish Economy.

- ❖ Since it is highly dependent on multinational investment, the tiger is not guaranteed for the future.

- ❖ Poverty, inequality, and long-term unemployment remain significant social problems.

- ❖ The Irish economy operates in an increasingly global context.

- ❖ Economic literacy is increasingly important to effective participation in union activity.

- ❖ In a capitalist economy, profits motivate most of the key economic decisions.

- ❖ Profits have their origin in the unpaid labour of working people.

- ❖ Corporations can pursue increasing profits using a variety of strategies.

- ❖ Even within areas of participation, workers still retain distinct interests, and need active union representation.

- ❖ In the context of the global economy, workers and their unions must co-operate and develop international solidarity.

- ❖ State policies have an important impact on working people's standard of living and ability to organise.

- ❖ The involvement of the trade union movement in the various national agreements has contributed to the growth in the Irish economy.

SECTION TWO

ACCOUNTING: KEEPING SCORE AND MEASURING PERFORMANCE

We live in a society where more and more of what we do is counted, measured and compared. The pressures created by the global economy mean that enterprises are constantly reviewing their profit performance. In the public sector, governments increasingly try to monitor activity in fields such as healthcare. They do this by using the sort of financial controls that have been developed for businesses.

In a society like this, it is important for workers as well as managers to understand accounting and financial information. It is particularly important because this information often doesn't give the full picture. Where decisions are based on arguments about financial effects, they are best challenged by those who understand what the financial statements leave in and leave out. In a world where accounting considerations are so significant, accounting is too important to be left to the accountants.

Section Two provides a picture of the sort of information that is contained in accounting reports. Chapter 4 discusses the various groups in society who use accounting information, and explains why accounting reports tend to focus on the needs of shareholders. Chapter 5 looks at the way in which a profit and loss account measures the performance of an enterprise. Chapter 6 discusses the balance sheet, which shows the financial position of an enterprise, and explains each of the major elements of this statement. Chapter 7 looks at how you can use the information in the accounts to analyse a company's performance and financial position. Chapter 8 reviews the various additional reports that are contained in the typical company's annual report.

In Chapter 9 the focus shifts to inside the business. Managers need information to run the enterprise. This chapter discusses the budget, which often plays a central role in planning and controlling the activities of the business.

Chapter 10 looks briefly at the idea that companies should report more about the environmental and social effects of their activities.

Chapter 4

Stakeholding: Who Has a Stake and Who Holds the Knowledge?

STAKEHOLDERS

In this chapter:

❖ **Who uses accounting information?**

❖ **Why do accounting reports focus on the interests of shareholders?**

❖ **How has accounting information recently become more publicly available?**

THE USERS OF ACCOUNTING INFORMATION

Enterprises are sometimes described as coalitions of different interest groups. In the case of a company trading for profit, accountants recognise several stakeholder groups as having a legitimate interest. Each stakeholder group is seen as a different "user" of accounting information.

The "user" viewpoint on financial statements comes from the recognition that these reports don't exist as an end in themselves. They are written to help people make decisions about companies they are interested in.

The American Accounting Association defines accounting as:

> *The process of identifying, measuring and communicating economic information to permit informed judgements and decisions by users of the information.*

Who are the User Groups?

The first statement in Ireland or Britain of this user (or stakeholder) perspective on financial reports came in a document called *The Corporate Report* (Accounting Standards Steering Committee, London, 1975). The user groups identified by that report are:

- **The equity investor group:** Shareholders in a company form the bulk of this group. This includes both the existing shareholders and those who might be considering making an investment in the future. Also included are those who have a right to buy shares in the future, like managers who are given stock options.

- **The loan creditor group:** Banks are the main members of this group, which also includes any other lenders to the company.

- **The employee group:** This includes present, retired and future employees. Existing employees look to the health of the company for their continuing employment. The present financial position of the company will be important information in deciding how capable the company is of paying for wage increases. Potential employees may be considering making a commitment to the company, perhaps by sacrificing their present job and its prospects. Former employees may be looking to the company for a pension.

- **The analyst-adviser group:** This group includes expert analysts like stockbrokers, who review company financial statements on behalf of their clients. Also included are trade union officials, who review them on behalf of employees, and journalists, whose interpretations are published in the newspapers and other periodicals.

- **The business contact group:** This consists of those involved in business dealings with the company, such as customers and suppliers.

- **The government:** The government has an interest as the tax authority. The government is also interested because of its role in managing the economy.

- **The public:** *The Corporate Report* paints this category in the broadest terms, "including taxpayers, ratepayers, consumers and other community and special interest groups such as political parties, consumer and environmental protection societies and regional pressure groups".

The General Purpose Report

The number of user groups and the variety of interests involved creates a problem in deciding what kind of information to provide. The trouble is made worse by the fact that there may also be considerable differences within the same general user group. Financial reporting is costly, involving the use of accountants and other professionals, as well as the actual costs of producing and distributing the report. Companies tend to concentrate on one report, which attempts to satisfy most of the information requirements of the different user groups. This is called a *general purpose report*.

Special Reports

Companies sometimes produce financial reports for specific user groups when necessary:

- Employees often have information requirements which are different from those of other groups. For example, employees will be interested in the particular location of jobs within the enterprise. Most other users will be interested only in the overall results of the enterprise's operations. Where those operations take place won't concern them. Thus, special reports may be produced for employees.

- Shareholders normally receive a single full annual report about the company. However, at times special reports must be prepared to inform shareholders' votes on decisions like mergers.

- A company looking for a substantial loan may approach a bank. The bank might make it a condition of granting the loan that the company provide it with specified financial information, both before the loan is made and afterwards, to enable the bank to monitor its investment.

THE FOCUS ON SHAREHOLDERS

Faced with the need to produce a general purpose report, it is not surprising that companies set about the task with a particular group in mind as the main group to be considered — the shareholders. Other groups can then be catered for by additions.

Why is the Focus so firmly on Shareholders?

Present company structures started to develop in the nineteenth century. As businesses got bigger, owners had to hire teams of managers. The managers' interests might be different from those of the owners, so the state stepped in to help maintain the owners' control. The law required the directors of a limited liability company to make an annual report to the shareholders. This annual report, in a phrase that is still widely used, was seen as "accounting for the stewardship" of the management. They had to explain what they had done with the money/capital entrusted to them, and how successful or unsuccessful they had been in making more money.

The annual report was initially seen as a defensive measure, protecting shareholders from possible abuse by an unaccountable management.

The idea that employees also needed protection — that their economic welfare was just as much or even more at the mercy of company managers and directors — did not occur to nineteenth-century legislators. The nineteenth century was not a time noted for its endorsement of the rights of labour. As these rights became increasingly recognised during the twentieth century, certain areas of the law failed to reflect this.

> *An English High Court decision of 1962 found that the directors of a company were not entitled to take into account the interests of its employees. This position was changed by legislation in Britain in 1980 and Ireland followed suit as recently as 1990. The issue demonstrates how the nineteenth century origins of company law cast a long shadow into the twentieth century.*

Annual Reports: Whose Perspective Counts?

Annual reports, then, emerged as a legal requirement that directors report to shareholders. The whole format of annual reports is influenced by this perspective. In annual reports, the company's performance is seen from the investors' perspective.

For instance, the wages paid to employees are treated as a cost, which must be deducted in arriving at a profit. From an alternative perspective, discussed in Section One, wages are not a cost, but the distribution of part of the net product created by labour in the production process.

Similarly, the interest paid on loans is treated as another cost. From the bank's perspective, it is a return to capital risked in much the same way as dividends paid to a shareholder are a return on the money invested.

ACCESS TO FINANCIAL INFORMATION

Which Users can actually obtain the Financial Information about a particular Company?

The answer to this crucial question is based partly on the law, partly on the power of economic groups to protect their interests, and partly on historical developments.

The discussion that follows considers the case of the limited liability company.

The Companies Act of 1963 is the major legislation dealing with the establishment and governance of companies in this country. It requires annual accounts to be sent to the "members" of the company. In the case of limited liability companies, those members are the shareholders. (The Act also requires annual accounts to be sent to the "debenture holders". Although there is no clear definition of who is covered by this term, it at least covers major lenders to the firm.)

Until 1986, the availability of financial information about companies was very restricted. There were exceptions. Public limited companies, generally those quoted on the Stock Exchange, were obliged by law to place their annual accounts on file with the Registrar of Companies. Once this was done, these accounts were available to the public. This rule, however, applied to a very small percentage of companies, less than one per cent of the total. Other companies (no matter what their size and economic and social significance) only had to report to shareholders and debenture holders. The "moral" rights of other important stakeholder or user groups were not recognised.

As a result of a Directive from the European Community, our law was changed in 1986 by the Companies (Amendment) Act. A more general requirement was introduced for filing financial information on the public record. The only major exception was companies not availing of limited liability.

> *On a sign in a car park attached to a large shop, part of a well-established chain, the company name now appears with the abbreviation "Ltd." painted out. This reflects the response of the company to the Companies (Amendment) Act, 1986. It had decided to become an unlimited company to avoid the disclosure requirements of the 1986 Act.*

This new legislation introduced rules for the publication of information, which depended on the size of companies. Some private companies (generally those companies which have a limited number of shareholders and are not quoted on a Stock Exchange) may be considered "small" or "medium-sized". This entitles them to file less information with the Registrar of Companies:

- Small private companies do not have to make a profit and loss account publicly available. This exemption allows these companies to avoid disclosing this information on their performance.

- Small and medium-sized companies are permitted to combine some of the sub-headings detailed in the *Profit and Loss Account* (covered in Chapter 5) and the *Balance Sheet* (covered in Chapter 6).

- Small and medium-sized companies are exempt from disclosing some of the information which large companies must include in *Notes to the Financial Statements* (covered in Chapter 8).

Who Tells the Story?

The credibility of any story depends on who is telling it. The same applies to financial statements. Who has the responsibility for telling the story appropriately? This is an important question about which there is often considerable confusion.

In the case of companies, the law makes it quite clear that the responsibility for the preparation of financial statements rests with the directors. They are appointed by the shareholders to run the company on their behalf and in their interests. This "accounting for stewardship" reflects the fact that shareholders have entrusted their capital to the directors. Obviously, all day-to-day recording of the company's activities, and putting together a set of financial statements, is actually done by accountants employed by the company for that purpose.

We shall see in later chapters how the process of preparing a set of financial statements requires many judgements. These judgements are ultimately the responsibility of the directors, regardless of the professional advice they take.

The annual accounts of companies have to be *audited* — that is, examined by independent accountants who then report to the shareholders on whether those accounts provide a true and fair view of their activities. Often these independent accountants will provide advice on how items should be measured, on how information should be disclosed, and on compliance with rules and regulations. However, the directors are still legally responsible.

Chapter 5

How the Accounts Measure Profit

In this chapter:

❖ **How do accounts measure the profit which a firm earns?**

❖ **How are costs calculated in some typical business situations?**

❖ **What sort of information is in a profit and loss account?**

❖ **How are profit figures sometimes misleading?**

INTRODUCTION

The financial statements of companies provide a range of information to their readers. This chapter focuses on profit — seen by many users, in particular shareholders, as the most important piece of information. Almost always, newspaper headlines report the percentage increase or decrease in the profit figure when companies publish their results.

The profit is shown in the financial statement known as the *profit and loss account*. The title reflects the fact that both profit and loss are a possibility. The examples in this chapter assume a positive profit.

The profit reported is the primary measurement of a company's performance, but it is an *accounting* measurement of performance. This means that certain important aspects of a company's performance may not be reflected in the figures.

For example, a company's employees might adopt a policy requiring new standards of customer service. This improves the company's reputation and will help to guarantee success in the future. But it won't show up in this year's profits.

MEASURING PROFIT

Profit measurement consists of two related steps:

* Measuring revenue

* Measuring costs/expenses.

First the company measures its *revenue*. In the case of a retailing or manufacturing company, this revenue is the value of the *sales* made during the period. In the case of a service company, revenue is measured as the amounts charged to customers for the services provided. (The term *turnover* is used in company financial statements to cover both types of revenue.)

Second, the company measures the *costs* or *expenses* incurred in the process of earning the revenue. Profit is calculated by deducting those costs and expenses from the revenue.

In a term used by accountants to describe this process, the costs are *matched* against the revenue they help to generate.

MEASURING REVENUE: THE ACCRUALS CONCEPT

The accruals concept is the important principle which accountants follow in calculating the revenue of a company.

The accruals concept requires that where a company sells goods to customers, revenue is measured as the value of sales made during a particular period, rather than the amount of money received from customers during that time. A sale made just before the end of a company's accounting period on 31 December will show up in the report for that period, even though cash will not be received until the following year. Indeed, sales are included as revenue in the measurement of profit, even though there is a risk that certain customers will never pay at all.

MEASURING COSTS

Calculating costs and expenses incurred while earning revenue is complicated. A whole range of difficulties emerges in practice.

For example, a retailing company regularly buys a product and re-sells it to its own customers. As a result of inflation, the price the company pays rises several times during the period of the report. This creates no problem if all the goods purchased have been re-sold. But what if some of those goods are unsold at the end of the financial period? The cost of those particular items can't be *matched* against the revenue of the period if a fair measurement of performance is to be achieved. How does the accountant determine the cost of the unsold items where prices have been changing at intervals during the year, when it is not possible to identify items individually? Accountants have a choice of possible approaches to take, and some of these are explained below.

Calculating the Cost of Sold and Unsold Items

A company makes the following purchases of a particular item of stock in which it is trading for the first time:

February	2,000 units	purchased at £5.00 each	£10,000
April	4,000 units	purchased at £5.50 each	22,000
June	4,000 units	purchased at £6.00 each	24,000
	10,000 units	purchased at a total cost of	£56,000

In August, 3,000 units are sold, and in October a further 4,000, leaving a closing stock of 3,000 units at the end of December. What is the cost of the 7,000 units sold and what is the cost of the remaining 3,000 units?

Under the first-in, first-out (FIFO) method, the cost of goods sold is *assumed* to be the cost of the earliest items purchased:

August	2,000 units at £5.00 each	£10,000
	1,000 units at £5.50 each	5,500
October	3,000 units at £5.50 each	16,500
	1,000 units at £6.00 each	6,000
		£38,000
Balance	3,000 units at £6.00 each	£18,000
	(note: FIFO = LILO, last-in, last-out)	

Under the last-in, first-out (LIFO) method, the cost of goods sold is *assumed* to be the cost of the latest items purchased:

August	3,000 units at £6.00 each	£18,000
October	1,000 units at £6.00 each	6,000
	3,000 units at £5.50 each	16,500
		£40,500
Balance	1,000 units at £5.50 each	£ 5,500
	2,000 units at £5.00 each	10,000
		£15,500

Under the weighted average method, the total cost of stock is averaged periodically over the number of units on hand, and the average is *assumed* to be the cost of goods sold:

August and	7,000 units at £5.60 each	£39,200
October	(£56,000/10,000 units)	
Balance	3,000 units at £5.60 each	£16,800

Measuring Depreciation

Another major problem in cost measurement arises from machinery and computer equipment that lasts for several years. Clearly, the measurement of a company's performance for a particular year would be misleading if the accountants deducted the whole cost of a new machine which was expected to earn revenue over, say, ten years. Accountants deal with this problem by deducting only a fraction of the total cost each year. This amount is called *depreciation.*

There are a number of different methods of calculating depreciation. Each of them shows the accountant applying the accruals concept, recognising costs at the time they are incurred by the use of the machinery. The most common methods are presented in the following example.

A company purchased machinery for £5,000. It expects to sell it for £2,048 after its useful economic life of four years. Depreciation on the *straight-line basis* is calculated as follows:

Original cost	£5,000
Estimated proceeds	2,048
Cost to be written off	£2,952
Annual depreciation	£738
(£2,952 divided by 4)	

An alternative method of depreciation is the *reducing balance* method, under which depreciation is a constant percentage of the original cost less accumulated depreciation to date. The figures in the illustration show a write down of the asset to £2,048 after four years using a depreciation rate of 20 per cent.

Original cost	£5,000
Depreciation — Year 1	1,000
	£4,000
Depreciation — Year 2	800
	£3,200
Depreciation — Year 3	640
	£2,560
Depreciation — Year 4	512
	£2,048

This illustration also shows how calculations of profit may be based on personal judgements made by those who prepare the financial statements. The amount of depreciation partly depends on how long the machinery is expected to last. This can't be known for certain in advance.

Measuring Other Costs

The *accruals* concept also lies behind a large number of other adjustments that accountants must make to their basic record of day-to-day transactions before they can produce a reliable set of financial statements. For example, a company pays annual rent shortly before the end of its financial reporting period.

Some of the money covers next year's rent. This part will have to be carried forward to the following financial period and charged against the revenue earned in that period. This and a similar problem are dealt with in the examples below.

The Accruals Concept

A company's accounting year ends on 31 December. It rents premises for three years from 1 October 2001 with rent of £6,000 payable annually in advance. On 31 December 2001, £4,500 of the first payment will be treated as a prepayment, the balance of £1,500 being the appropriate cost to match against the revenue in the profit and loss account of 2001. The prepayment of £4,500, which has secured the use of the premises for the nine months from 1 January 2002 to 30 September 2002, will be matched against the revenue earned in the next year ended 31 December 2002.

The same company received electricity bills of £1,200 for the two-month period October–November 2001 and of £1,000 for the period December 2001 – January 2002. Assuming that the first of these had been paid by 31 December 2001, additional electricity costs of £500 (half of £1,000) would be accrued and charged at that date. If the bill for December 2001 – January 2002 had not yet been received at the time the annual financial statements were being prepared, and a meter reading was not available, an estimate might be made on the basis of the October–November bill, or the corresponding bill for December 2000 – January 2001, or both.

THE FORMAT OF THE PROFIT AND LOSS ACCOUNT

Directors and accountants must present information in a way that is most useful to those reading the financial statements. For companies, this process includes following standard formats that are laid down by company legislation. The Companies (Amendment) Act, 1986, offers companies a choice between different formats, one of which must be chosen and followed consistently in the company's annual financial statements. The most popular format in Ireland is used as the basis for the presentation in the **Profit and Loss Account** below. The various headings are explained in the sections that follow.

Figure 9: Profit and Loss Account

	£000s	£000s
Turnover		18,325
Cost of sales		(12,869)
Gross profit		5,456
Distribution costs	537	
Administrative expenses	1,142	
		(1,679)
Operating profit		3,777
Other income		78
Profit before interest payable		3,855
Interest payable		(472)
Profit before taxation		3,383
Tax on profit on ordinary activities		(463)
Profit after taxation		2,920
Minority interest		(180)
Profit for the financial year		2,740
Dividends paid	398	
Dividends proposed	993	
		(1,391)
Retained profit		1,349
Profit or loss brought forward at the beginning of the year		8,982
Profit or loss carried forward at the end of the year		10,331

Turnover, Cost of Sales, Gross Profit

In the case of a retailer, cost of sales will consist of the cost of the items purchased from suppliers and subsequently resold to their own customers.

In the case of a manufacturer, the calculation of cost of sales is more complex. In calculating the cost of manufacturing its products, a company must include the cost of raw materials used and the cost of labour employed in that process. It must also include all the additional costs of manufacturing such as the depreciation of machinery, the cost of maintaining a factory (including the costs of lighting and heating), and the cost of providing power for the machines.

Deducting cost of sales from turnover gives a figure known as *gross profit*. This is an important indicator of a fundamental aspect of company profitability. From this gross profit other costs must be deducted.

GROSS PROFITS

Distribution Costs

Distribution costs reflect the cost of distributing the product to the organisation's customers, whether these are the wages and salaries paid to employees involved in this process, the costs (including depreciation) of vehicles used in distribution, or any other costs incurred for this purpose.

Businesses sell goods to customers on credit (recall that revenue from sales is recognised immediately those sales take place). When customers fail to pay the company, the amounts that cannot be recovered are referred to as bad debts, and these are included in distribution costs. The directors must use their judgement in estimating the bad debts *expected* as a result of sales. They must try to anticipate how much of the money owed to them by their customers (referred to as debtors in the financial statements) will not be paid. It is a difficult task. Typically, directors look at problematic debts individually. These would include debts that have been outstanding for a long time and debts that are disputed by the customer, perhaps because the quality of the product wasn't satisfactory. Provision must also be made for the possibility of failing to recover debts where there is no apparent difficulty at present. This is usually done by taking a percentage of the debtors figure.

Administrative Expenses

Administrative expenses are also deducted from the gross profit. These include the wages and salaries paid to those working in the office, the depreciation of computers and other office equipment, the cost of stationery, the cost of renting premises to be used by office staff, and so on.

The classification of costs between the various headings is not always easy. For instance, premises may be rented and used partly for manufacturing, partly for distribution, partly for administration, with the proportion varying from time to time.

How should supermarkets classify the cost of employing people to stack shelves? Is that part of the cost of sales or is it part of distribution costs? Often there is no "right" answer to these questions. What is important is that individual companies are consistent in how they answer these questions, so that their progress from one year to the next can be easily judged. Also, accountants as a professional group may develop a way of interpreting a phrase such as "distribution costs" which is generally accepted. Absolute consistency and absolute uniformity are, however, virtually impossible to achieve.

Operating Profit

This is an important measure of performance, which is not part of the format but is provided by most companies. It shows the result of the basic trading transactions of the company.

Other Income

Other types of income arise from shares in other companies and other forms of investment. The legal format includes five lines for such income, but these have not been shown in the illustration. In the case of many companies, this kind of income will either not arise at all or be fairly insignificant.

Since investments may lose value, the legal format also includes a line to recognise the amounts written off to reflect such losses.

Profit before Interest Payable

Where other types of income arise, many companies add them to the operating profit to calculate a sub-total for *profit before interest payable*, another widely used measure of performance. It enables users to compare two companies where one has borrowed heavily and the other has not.

Interest Payable

This is the amount of interest the company had to pay on its own debts. Since many firms borrow a large part of the finance they require, this is often a significant part of the company's profit and loss account. Interest is deducted to give the company's profit before taxation.

Taxation

Corporation tax is based on the amount of profit the company makes. But deducting tax is not simply a question of applying the tax rate to the profits calculated by the company. This is partly because of the personal judgement involved in the calculation of profits.

Depreciation, for example, is the result of many "guesses" by the company directors about things like the expected useful life of the company assets. Rather than giving the company the right to deduct whatever it thinks is appropriate, the law requires a system of *capital allowances* to be used in place of the cost of depreciation. This system of capital allowances ensures fairness between different companies. It also creates a situation where the capital allowances system can be used as an instrument of economic policy. If, for instance, lawmakers think that companies should be encouraged to expand by investing in new plant and machinery, then they make the capital allowances more generous.

Companies show the amount of profits both before and after the deduction of taxation. The effect of taxation may differ between companies. Manufacturing companies, for instance, have been paying tax at lower rates in recent years.

Minority Interest

A **minority interest** may arise where one company makes a significant investment in another. Where such an investment is significant enough to give the investor control of the investee (typically where more than 50 per cent of the shares are owned), *group accounts* must be prepared. Where the company has not purchased 100 per cent of the subsidiary, the remainder will be owned by other people, the minority shareholders. The share of the profits belonging to them is the minority interest.

Extraordinary and Exceptional Items

Several headings in the standard format (not shown in the illustration) refer to what might be described as "extraordinary items". These arise from efforts to deal with unusual items. Certain unusual items, if included in the calculation of profit, might not give a true picture of the underlying performance of the company.

> *A company makes a profit of £5 million in 2000. It reports a profit for 2001 of £7 million. It seems that the company has improved its performance and that the directors are to be congratulated. However, the real story turns out to be that the company has made a profit from its day-to-day trading activities of only £4 million, compared to last year's figure of £5 million. A once-off profit on the sale of land purchased in 1947 for £10,000 and now sold for £3,000,000 has hidden the underlying decline.*

In line with accounting's *realisation principle*, such profits are recognised not when the assets increase in value, but when they are *realised*, that is, sold for cash or on credit. In the case of the sale of land, no profit will have been recognised in the past because of uncertainty about the value of the land and the possibility of future declines in value. Directors and accountants may be able to estimate the gain in value reasonably closely, but the underlying concept of *prudence* prevents them from recognising it as profit. When goods and services are sold in the normal course of business, we know exactly how the value of the goods and services should be determined.

The unusual nature of the £3 million arising from the sale of land suggests that it should be left out of the calculation of the annual profit in the above example. It is, however, the directors of a company who have responsibility for preparing the annual financial statements. Since they are the people who decide what is unusual, they may exercise their discretion in a way that makes them look good. Directors may be tempted to include unusual gains by stretching the definition of "usual" as widely as possible. They may also be tempted to exclude losses wherever they can make any sort of case, no matter how unconvincing, that they are "unusual".

ER... UNDER EXTRAORDINARY ITEMS?

To deal with this problem, the accounting profession decided in 1974 to classify gains and losses that arose from events outside the company's normal activities as "extraordinary". These items had to be excluded from the calculation of profit from ordinary activities, and then brought into the profit and loss account under the "extraordinary" headings. If there were additional unusual items — which might be misleading because, for instance, they were unusually large — then these had to be disclosed as well.

> *A major customer of a company goes out of business, owing the company a large amount of money. This is not an "extraordinary" event. Customers often go bankrupt. The accounting profession's solution is to require these items to be included in the measurement of profit from ordinary activities, but to insist on clear disclosure of such big items to prevent users from being misled. Items of this nature are described as "exceptional" items.*

Unfortunately, the 1974 solution to the problem of unusual items didn't work in practice.

Because of the difficulty of defining, in a complex business world, what was normal and what was not, directors retained a considerable amount of discretion and flexibility. Many believed that directors were too willing to classify as extraordinary negative items that would reflect badly on their performance, while happily classifying as merely exceptional positive items that would reflect well. Although both exceptional and extraordinary items did ultimately end up in the profit and loss account, negative extraordinary items were only brought in at the final stage. Crucially, this was after the calculation of *earnings per share* (essentially the profit of the company divided by the number of shares). This is a key indicator used by stock markets.

After a series of unsuccessful attempts to distinguish the extraordinary from the merely exceptional, the accounting rules were amended to include a definition of ordinary activities so wide that every conceivable aspect of a company's affairs was included. As a result, there was nothing left to be classified as "extraordinary". These lines in the standard format are now basically redundant.

Ordinary activities are now defined as:

> *Any activities which are undertaken by a reporting entity as part of its business and such related activities in which the entity engages in furtherance of, incidental to, or arising from, these activities. Ordinary activities* **include the effects** *on the reporting entity* **of any event in the various environments** *in which it operates, including the political, regulatory, economic and geographic environments,* **irrespective of the frequency or unusual nature of the events.**

Some key phrases have been highlighted to emphasise that this definition is wide enough to include the effects of, for instance:

- a political coup, involving nationalisation of an overseas subsidiary company

- an earthquake.

The effective abolition of extraordinary items means that additional importance is now attached to the identification and disclosure of exceptional items. The disclosure requirements are not apparent from the standard format reproduced in the **Profit and Loss Account** (Figure 9, page 62). They are imposed in rules developed by the accounting profession.

Exceptional items are defined as:

> *Material items which derive from events or transactions that fall within the ordinary activities of the reporting entity and which individually or, if of a similar type, in aggregate, need to be disclosed by virtue of their size or incidence if the financial statements are to give a true and fair view.*

In some cases, exceptional items must be disclosed in the profit and loss account. They would appear after the calculation of operating profit and before the calculation of profit before interest payable. These items are:

- Profits or losses on the sale or closure of an operation

- Costs of a fundamental reorganisation or restructuring

- Profits or losses on the sale of fixed assets.

Profit for the Financial Year

After all the deductions discussed above have been made, the company calculates the overall profit for the financial year. This is the final measure of performance that the profit and loss account shows.

Dividends

The fact that the profit and loss account is presented from the perspective of the shareholder has already been discussed. That perspective means that when the company pays or proposes to pay dividends to its shareholders, the dividends constitute what is called an *appropriation* of profit. They are not a cost that must be deducted in arriving at the profit.

> *One profitable company in a declining industry decides that large cash dividends should be paid to its shareholders, since the company cannot itself find profitable ways of using this money. Another profitable company in an expanding industry decides to pay no dividend at all to its shareholders, since it has very profitable ways of re-investing the money. It makes no sense to regard the former company as less profitable, simply because the retained profits, after the payment of dividends, are lower.*

Deducting dividends from the profit for the year gives a figure of *retained profit*. This is then added to the figure of retained profits from all the previous years of the company's life, called the profit brought forward at the beginning of the year. This gives the profit carried forward at the end of the year. Such accumulated profits remain available for paying dividends to shareholders.

SOME SHORTCOMINGS OF THE PROFIT AND LOSS ACCOUNT

It is important to remember that the profit and loss account is partly the result of applying certain accounting conventions. Given the complexities and uncertainties of the business world, this sometimes produces unsatisfactory results.

A company makes three payments in relation to advertising costs in 2000. The first payment of £10,000 in January is for a one-off event taking place in March 2000. Clearly, the whole of the cost should be charged against the revenues arising from that event. The third payment in December 2000 is for another one-off event to take place in February 2001. It is appropriate to regard this payment as a prepayment, to carry it forward to match against the revenues in 2001, and thus to omit it from the profit and loss account of 2000. But what of the second payment, an amount of £30,000 paid in October and November 2000, for an advertising campaign which was intended to make the company's products known to a wider range of customers? Management expects that this campaign will increase sales in 2001 and probably even afterwards.

The accruals concept or matching principle might suggest that part at least of this advertising cost should be carried forward to be matched against the revenues of later years. However, the accruals concept is subordinate to the prudence concept, whereby revenue and profits are not anticipated, but are recognised by inclusion in the profit and loss account only when realised in the form of cash or credit sales.

The principle of matching is appropriate only so long as the relationship between revenue and costs can be established clearly. In the case of the advertising costs of £30,000, the relationship between those costs and any future revenues is, whatever the directors may hope, uncertain. There is no alternative but to treat the payment as a cost of the year in which it was incurred.

Similar difficulties may arise in other areas. Research and development projects may promise substantial benefits for a company in the future. Nevertheless, there will be too much uncertainty to allow research and development expenditure to be safely carried forward to a later year. Accounting rules in this area provide that all research expenditure must be charged to the profit and loss account in the year in which it takes place. Development expenditure may be carried forward only when certain stringent conditions, designed to ensure that a profitable product is not far from its launch, have been satisfied.

Paradoxically, these rules mean that in certain cases, a company doing the right things — investing in new product development, undertaking advertising to increase its future profitability, investing in staff and management training — may report smaller profits than a similar company resting on its laurels. In the medium to long term, the former company should prosper and report enhanced profits, while the latter company is likely to decline and report lower profitability. However, the possibility exists for users to be misled in the short term. The degree to which this is a problem may depend on the ability of management to explain what is going on, and whether they are believable in the light of their past explanations.

Chapter 6

Reporting the Financial Position

In this chapter:

❖ **What sort of information is in a balance sheet?**

❖ **What are assets, liabilities, and capital?**

❖ **What are group accounts?**

THE BALANCE SHEET

Annual performance is often seen as the most important aspect of financial reporting, but other factors are also vital to understanding the company. Knowing how well a company has performed in the recent past does not directly tell us anything about the company's overall financial position. For information on this aspect of a company's financial affairs, we must turn to the *balance sheet* (called, in the USA, the statement of financial position).

The balance sheet consists of three major elements.

- **Assets**

- **Liabilities**

- **Capital/owner's equity** (in the case of a company, usually referred to as *shareholders' funds*).

The **Balance Sheet** example below is based on Format 1 under the Companies (Amendment) Act, 1986. This is the most common format of the two available to companies under the legislation. The most significant elements are discussed in the immediately following sections. A fuller analysis of the elements is presented later in the chapter.

Figure 10: The Balance Sheet

	£000s	£000s	£000s
Fixed assets			
Intangible assets			
Patents and trademarks	105		
Goodwill	2,683		
		2,788	
Tangible assets			
Land and buildings	3,053		
Plant and machinery	7,298		
Fixtures, fittings, tools and equipment	1,004		
		11,355	
Financial assets		543	
			14,686
Current assets			
Stocks			
Raw materials and consumables	1,864		
Work in progress	114		
Finished goods and goods for resale	3,802		
		5,780	
Debtors			
Trade debtors	2,856		
Prepayments and accrued income	982		
		3,838	
Investments		1,035	
Cash at bank and in hand		2,180	
		12,833	

Creditors: amounts falling due within one year		
Debenture loans	100	
Bank loans and overdrafts	217	
Trade creditors	4,291	
Other creditors including tax and social welfare	469	
Accruals and deferred income	167	
Proposed dividends	993	
		6,237
Net current assets		6,596
Total assets less current liabilities		21,282
Creditors: amounts falling due after more than one year		
Debenture loans	1,900	
Bank loans and overdrafts	2,570	
		4,470
Provisions for liabilities and charges		
Deferred taxation	62	
Other provisions	40	
		102
		(4,572)
		16,710
Capital and reserves		
Called up share capital		3,280
Share premium account		1,062
Revaluation reserve		849
Other reserves		103
Profit and loss account		10,331
		15,625
Minority interest		1,085
		16,710

ASSETS

Asset is a term in everyday use, and there is little difference between its everyday meaning and its more technical meaning to accountants. In simple terms, *assets* are what the company owns. They can be either *fixed assets* or *current assets*.

Fixed Assets

Machinery and computer equipment, discussed in the previous chapter in relation to depreciation, are examples of what are known as *fixed assets*. They last a number of years and are held for continuing use in the business. Things like machines are known as *tangible fixed assets* because they can be seen and touched.

Companies also sometimes own *intangible fixed assets*, such as patents, which aren't physical assets.

Financial fixed assets arise where a company makes an investment in another company, such as by buying shares in that company or lending money to it.

Current Assets

In contrast to fixed assets, current assets are not held for continuing use in the business. They consist of things that are constantly replaced as part of the day-to-day operating activities of the enterprise. They mainly comprise:

- **Stocks**

- **Debtors**

- **Cash**

Stocks represent items purchased for re-sale, materials bought for use in the company's own manufacturing operations, goods manufactured by a company and held for sale to its customers, and goods in the process of manufacture.

Debtors represents money owed to the company by customers. In Chapter 5 on the Profit and Loss Account, it was explained that revenue is measured when sales take place, even though the cash has not yet been collected. When the accounting system records the sale, it simultaneously records the amount due from the customer as a debtor. Later, when the customer pays the sum due, the amount of debtors is reduced, and the amount of cash increased.

Cash is a word which is used in a number of different ways by accountants. For present purposes, it is useful to give the full description that the companies legislation requires for the balance sheet:

Cash at bank and in hand.

This includes:

- Current accounts with a bank

- Short-term deposit accounts

- Notes and coins kept on the company's premises.

LIABILITIES

The next major balance sheet category is *liabilities*. Liabilities are what the company owes. Some examples follow.

- A company borrows from the bank. The company has an obligation to repay the loan. This obligation appears in the balance sheet as a liability.

- A company acquires stocks on credit (no immediate cash payment is made) from another company. The amount due to the other company is a liability. (The supplier to whom the company owes an obligation is known as its *creditor*.)

- A company asks its employees to work overtime just before the end of its financial year. The payments for this overtime work will not be calculated until the following year. The amount due will appear in the balance sheet at the end of the year as an *accrual*, another form of liability.

- Tax and PRSI deducted from employees under the PAYE system, which will shortly be paid over to the Revenue Commissioners, represents a liability in the period between its deduction from the employees' gross wages and its payment to the Revenue.

- As a final illustration, the dividend which the directors decide to pay to the company's shareholders on the basis of the profits earned is shown as a liability in the balance sheet at the end of the year (even though it may be some time before the dividends are paid).

In presenting the balance sheet, liabilities of a company must be divided into those due within one year of the balance sheet date (often called current liabilities) and those due after more than one year. This is an important division in assessing the strength of a company's financial position. Excessive short-term liabilities may threaten a company's survival in the immediate future even if other aspects of its financial position and performance appear good.

The format of the balance sheet helps to show why this division is important. From the total of current assets (generally, items that will be turned into cash in the course of trading within a year), the total of the short-term creditors or current liabilities is deducted. This gives the amount of *net current assets*. The higher this figure is, the safer the company's financial position. Investors and other users often look at this relationship between current assets and current liabilities in judging a company's stability.

The figure for net current assets is added to the total for fixed assets to give *total assets less current liabilities*. The remainder of the balance sheet shows where the finance for the total assets less current liabilities has come from. Partly it comes from long-term creditors, listed as *creditors: amounts falling due after more than one year*. Partly it comes from shareholders' funds, discussed below.

Shareholders' Funds

The last of the major balance sheet categories is the most difficult to understand. The position is complicated by the fact that it is described by various different names, which depend partly on the type of firm producing the financial statements. For limited companies, the category is often referred to as *shareholders' funds*, though, as can be seen from the Balance Sheet, the Companies Act heading for this category is *capital and reserves*. The easiest way to explain this category is to look at its contents on an item-by-item basis.

Called up share capital

When companies start life, they raise their initial funds by selling shares. In return for their money, shareholders get part ownership of the undertaking. Each share has a nominal or face value, typically £1 per share, though it might be 50p or 5p.

Not all of the nominal value of the shares may be called for immediately. The company directors may plan to begin operations in two phases, and allow the shareholders to pay, say, half of the nominal or face value initially, with the rest expected to be called up some months later. This explains the need to refer in the balance sheet to *called up* share capital.

Share Premium Account

When a company has been in existence for several years, its shares may have increased in value above the original amount subscribed. This may be partly because the company has earned profits by successful trading, and reinvested the money in expanding the business.

It may also be regarded as worth more because it has demonstrated the ability to trade profitably or is seen as having some quality (such as a high quality labour force) that gives it an enhanced value. This value, incidentally, does *not* appear on the balance sheet or elsewhere in the financial statements of the company. Accountants refer to the "book value" of a company, meaning the amount of recorded assets minus liabilities. This will usually be less, sometimes a lot less, than the economic value of the company.

When a company needs to raise additional money, it would not be fair to existing shareholders if the new shares were issued at the same price as the initial shares. Consequently, the new shares will be issued at a *premium*, this premium reflecting the additional amount charged over the face value. This amount must be entered into the *share premium account*, the next balance sheet item under *capital and reserves*.

A company commences its life by issuing 200,000 shares at their nominal value of £1 each. After three years, the company decides that it needs to raise a further amount of capital in the region £300,000 to £400,000. It is estimated that the company's value has grown from the initial £200,000 to £360,000, so that each share is currently worth £1.80.

The company cannot reasonably issue shares to new shareholders at the original price of £1. For instance, if it issued 360,000 shares at £1 each, the original shareholders would have contributed the existing company, presently worth £360,000, to the enlarged company. The new shareholders would also have contributed exactly the same value, £360,000, in the form of cash.

But the new shareholders would own 360,000 shares in the enlarged company (64 per cent) while the original shareholders would hold 200,000 shares (36 per cent). The new shareholders would be entitled to 64 per cent of any profits distributed and to 64 per cent of the company's assets in the event that the company was dissolved. This is obviously unfair.

The solution is for the company to issue 200,000 shares at a premium of £0.80 per share, that is, at a total price of £1.80. Then both groups of shareholders would have contributed equal value to the enlarged company, the original shareholders contributing a business presently worth £360,000 and the new shareholders £360,000 in cash. Furthermore, each group would own 50 per cent of the shares, and would therefore share equally in any profits distributed in the future and in assets distributed on the winding up of the company.

The capital and reserves section of the balance sheet of the company would record the effect of these two sets of transactions as follows:

Called up share capital	£400,000
Share premium account	160,000
	£560,000

Revaluation Reserve

When a company acquires an asset it is recorded at the purchase price. In most cases, an asset will continue to be shown in the annual financial statements at this purchase price until it is sold. Tangible fixed assets are shown at their original purchase price, less the amounts charged as depreciation.

Occasionally, however (usually in relation to land and buildings), a company will revalue a fixed asset and reflect that revaluation in its balance sheet. Any additional value arising from such a revaluation must be included in the *revaluation reserve*. It is forbidden by company law to include this additional value in the profit and loss account. It does not represent an actually realised profit, and it is usually surrounded by a significant degree of uncertainty.

Other Reserves

These arise relatively infrequently in practice, and are technical in nature. We won't deal with them here.

Profit and Loss Account

The *profit and loss account* figure that follows represents all the profits earned by the company since its start, minus the amounts paid out as dividends to the shareholders. (It is the amount described in Chapter 5 as the *profit carried forward at the end of the year*.) For profitable and well-established companies, this figure may be very significant indeed.

Companies frequently choose not to pay out a large proportion of their profits to the shareholders, preferring to reinvest the available funds in an expansion of activities that promise further profits (and ultimately larger dividends) in the future. This increases the value of shares (since the additional activity and the related profits mean that the company is worth more). This gives the shareholder a capital gain to add to the cash dividend received. If the company's policy is well chosen, the combined return to shareholders may exceed the return that would be available if the full amount of profits had been given out as dividends.

Minority Interest

This line appears below the capital and reserves section of the balance sheet and is explained below in connection with *Group Accounts*.

WHY THE ACCOUNTS BALANCE

The accounts will always balance because there is an underlying "accounting equation". This can be presented in two forms:

Assets – Liabilities = Capital, or

Assets = Liabilities + Capital

Some examples will show how every transaction leaves the two sides of the equation in balance:

- When shareholders subscribe cash in return for shares, both assets and capital increase by the same amount.

- When stocks are purchased on credit, both assets and liabilities go up by the same amount.

- When cash is used to purchase fixed assets, one type of asset increases, another decreases.

- When cash is used to pay creditors, assets decrease and liabilities decrease by the same amount.

- When successful trading takes place, assets increase and capital (through the balance on the profit and loss account) increases by the same amount; for example, if an item of stock is bought for £20 cash and re-sold for £30 cash, the asset cash will increase by £10, exactly the amount by which the profit (and thus the capital) goes up.

SUB-HEADINGS EXPLAINED

This chapter has so far reviewed the major elements included in the balance sheet, dealing with assets, liabilities, and the third area of importance, shareholders' funds. This final section of the chapter explains some of the more important sub-headings in the balance sheet format. Not all of these were included in Figure 10 on pages 76–77.

Intangible and Tangible Fixed Assets

Because of the physical nature of the assets involved, the sub-headings under *tangible fixed assets* are self-explanatory. The sub-headings under *intangible fixed assets* are more difficult to understand.

In the previous chapter, some of the difficulties of measuring performance were discussed. One of these was accounting for the fact that companies will often spend money on research and development. We saw that in most cases these costs will be charged to the profit and loss account in the year in which the money was spent. Subject to certain strict conditions, however, *development costs* may be carried forward as an asset in the balance sheet. None are included in the illustration.

Companies will often have the right to exploit an invention through a *patent*, or the right to benefit from the use of a well-established trade name through a *trademark*. If these have been purchased from another company, the cost will appear in the balance sheet, after whatever depreciation (called *amortisation* in the case of intangible fixed assets) is necessary. Amortisation of a patent, for example, must clearly recognise the limited time period over which the law will grant exclusive rights for the exploitation of an invention.

Goodwill

When one company purchases another, it pays a price reflecting the worth of that other company. That worth in turn will reflect the profits that the other company is expected to earn in the future. These will depend not just on the assets that appear in that company's balance sheet, but on a range of other factors which are harder to pin down. They include such factors as a high quality labour force and a high quality management team, which make a company worth more than a comparable company with exactly the same balance sheet assets. They often include the existence of brand names. When one company purchases another and the price paid reflects the existence of such factors, the excess paid over the value of the balance sheet assets is known as *goodwill*.

When a company has created its own goodwill, or developed its own brands, it might wish to include them in the balance sheet at an estimate of their value. However, present accounting rules generally prevent goodwill, or the value of any brand names, from being added to the balance sheet except when they arise on the purchase of another company.

The debate on how to account for goodwill has been raging for more than a hundred years. Complex rules recently introduced require the goodwill of a purchased company to be included in the balance sheet and usually amortised (depreciated) over a useful economic life of not more than 20 years.

There are no headings for such valuable factors in a company's makeup as good staff relations and a good reputation with customers. Expenditure in these areas will reduce the company's reported profit in the short term, but should bring long-term benefits. The value of these benefits will be recognised in financial statements as goodwill only when one company purchases another. Such expenditure does not create an asset in the accounts of the company spending the money on its reputation.

Financial Assets

Seven different sub-headings are listed under financial fixed assets. These are:

1. Shares in group undertakings

2. Loans to group undertakings

3. Interest in associated undertakings

4. Other participating interests

5. Loans to undertakings in which a participating interest is held

6. Other investments other than loans

7. Other loans.

To understand them we must explain group companies. Most large industrial and commercial organisations operate not through a single company but through a group of companies. This means that one company, called either the parent company (*parent undertaking*) or the holding company, has one or more subsidiary companies (*subsidiary undertaking*).

There is a complex set of rules for defining a *subsidiary*, each involving a different way of gaining control over another company. Nevertheless, in the vast majority of cases, control is achieved simply by owning more than 50 per cent of the shares of the other company. Ownership of more than half of the shares gives the owner the power to elect the board of directors. Since the board of directors run the company, control is achieved.

Because of the close relationship between parent and subsidiary, the law provides for separate disclosure of the results of financial transactions between them.

Shares in group undertakings shows the cost of the parent's investment in shares of subsidiaries. (It might also include investment in a fellow subsidiary when both companies have a common parent.) They are recorded under financial fixed assets if, as will normally be the case, it is intended to keep the investment indefinitely. They appear under current asset investments if there is an intention to sell off the investment soon after it is bought (as might happen where a group of companies is acquired but one company in that group is not wanted).

Under financial fixed assets, we also find *loans to group undertakings*.

Accounting and the law are also interested in seeing that useful information is provided in cases where there is a shareholding which is large enough to be significant but without giving control. The first term to understand in this context is *participating interest*. This is a shareholding held in another company in order to get benefits through exercising influence on the other company.

Where the shareholding is not large enough to make the investor a parent, but large enough to give it *significant influence* over the other company's policy, the other company is said to be an *associated undertaking*. Generally, this happens where the shareholding amounts to something between 20 per cent and 50 per cent of the company's share capital.

A company with surplus cash and a belief that stock market values are about to rise might invest that cash in the short term in shares of such major Irish companies as CRH, AIB and Bank of Ireland. The investments amount to such a small proportion of the share capital of those companies that no question of influence over them arises. These will be classified as *other investments other than loans*. However, such investments will be included under fixed assets only if it is planned to hold them on a continuing basis; if they are purchased for the short term, then they will be classified under current assets.

The category for *other loans* likewise relates to loans to enterprises where no participating interest is held.

Current Assets

Stocks

A manufacturing company purchases *raw materials*. In the case of a furniture manufacturer, these would include wood, sheets of hardboard and hinges. It will also purchase *consumables*, such as oil for lubricating the machines during the manufacturing process. At any particular point in time, the company will hold a stock of these items, and these will usually appear in the balance sheet at their cost. (Applying the *prudence* concept to the area of stock results in a rule that each item of stock is valued at price paid or *net realisable value*, whichever is lower. Net realisable value is the amount that would be received if the item were sold.)

When the company has completed the manufacturing process, the products made and not yet sold are classified as *finished goods* and included at the cost to make them or the net realisable value, whichever is lower. Where the company has goods in the course of manufacture, the cost of these items is included as *work in progress*.

Where a company acquires the products which it sells, not by manufacture, but by purchasing them from a supplier, any unsold items of this type are *goods for resale*.

Debtors

Trade debtors represent the amounts owed by customers. Trade debtors are recorded initially at the full amount of the sales value. Any subsequent payments of cash by the customer will reduce the amount owed.

When a company prepares a balance sheet it must also consider the possibility that a particular customer may not be able or willing to pay. Where a company is fairly certain that a debt will prove uncollectible, it writes off the amount as a bad debt. It ceases to recognise the amount owed as an asset, and transfers it instead to the profit and loss account, where it represents a cost of doing business on credit terms.

Where there is doubt as to a debt's collectibility, a provision is established. This provision is deducted from the amount owed in the balance sheet, and also becomes part of the overall charge in the profit and loss account for *bad and doubtful debts*. This will only be shown separately where the amount is exceptional. To allow for the likelihood of unidentified problems in the collection of debts, companies usually establish a general provision, calculated as a percentage of debtors, to supplement the specific provisions they make for known difficulties.

Under the *accruals* and *matching* concepts, costs are not recognised when they are paid, but in the period in which they are incurred. For example, a payment of six months' rent at the beginning of December is not all included in the profit and loss account of that year. Instead, one-sixth of it is included for the December rent. The balance, which gives the company the right to use the premises in the following year, is included in the balance sheet as a *prepayment*.

Such prepayments arise in many areas of a company's activities, insurance and road tax being two familiar examples.

Another element included under the general heading of debtors is *accrued income*. Here are some examples.

- A company places surplus cash in a bank deposit account. That cash earns interest from the day of deposit, even though the bank may not have to pay the interest until the end of the deposit term. Companies calculate the interest earned up to the balance sheet date and include it as *accrued income*.

- Other examples would include interest on government bonds and dividends on shares owned by the company that are declared but not yet paid.

Investments

Stocks, debtors and cash are the three main types of current assets. Some companies will also have *investments* held as current assets. It is interesting to note that these might consist of shares in other companies, which were previously referred to under the heading of financial fixed assets. What distinguishes the two categories is the intention with which the assets are held.

If surplus cash is invested in some shares of a major company, in the hope that the value will grow in the few months before the funds are required for the investing company's own purposes such as purchasing new machinery, then the investment is a current asset. If one company takes a 20 per cent interest in another and plans to retain that interest indefinitely, then that investment is a fixed asset.

Creditors

Debenture loans are long-term loans normally acknowledged by the issue of a bond. Although they are long term, they often involve repayment in instalments, which means that part of a debenture loan may fall under the heading *creditors: amounts falling due within one year.*

Bank loans and overdrafts are self-explanatory.

Trade creditors represent the amounts owed to suppliers on account of goods and services provided and not yet paid for.

Accruals arise where an expense has been incurred but not yet paid in cash. Examples would be electricity used, rent where the payments are made in arrears and not in advance, and overtime payments due to employees.

Deferred income has been received but not yet earned. Some examples follow.

- A company owns premises which it rents out, and the rental payments on those premises are received in advance, but the company must bring into its profit and loss account only the amount of rentals that have actually been earned by the balance sheet date. The proportion of the rental payment that relates to the following financial period will be included as *deferred income*.

- Another common example often shown separately is *government grants*. Governments sometimes encourage investment in fixed assets by giving cash grants to companies. The grants are used to purchase fixed assets. The cost of the fixed assets will be spread as depreciation charges in the company's profit and loss account over the whole useful life of the assets. When the cash received from the government goes into the bank account, a matching amount is included in deferred income. This is transferred to the profit and loss account over the life of the assets in a pattern exactly mirroring that of the depreciation charges. The amount transferred is deducted from the expense heading under which the related depreciation is charged; where the grant relates to fixed assets used in manufacturing, for example, both the depreciation and the grant transferred will be included under cost of sales. The amount not yet transferred is shown as *deferred income*.

Provisions for Liabilities and Charges

Most companies meet their pension obligations by establishing a separate pension fund for their employees. Such a fund will not appear on the company's balance sheet. However, if a company doesn't have a pension fund, it must include its *pension obligations* on its balance sheet.

In addition to tax arising immediately as a result of its activities, a company may need to establish a more long-term provision. Often, a significant element in such a provision is that for what is called *deferred taxation*.

This arises because instead of allowing deductions for depreciation, the government permits the deduction of what are termed *capital allowances*.

At times, to encourage more investment in fixed assets, the rate deducted for capital allowances may be much bigger than the corresponding depreciation charges. This means that in the years immediately following the acquisition of fixed assets, the taxable profits are lower than the accounting profits. But in later years, the opposite will be the case: taxable profits will be higher than the accounting profits as the capital allowances for tax purposes are used up and the depreciation charges continue to be deducted from the revenue by the accountants.

Accountants deal with this timing problem by including a provision in the balance sheet for the taxation that has been deferred in this way to later years.

GROUP ACCOUNTS

An important consequence of the existence of a parent-subsidiary relationship is the requirement to produce *group accounts*.

The directors of a parent company must produce, in addition to the accounts of their own company, a set of accounts which consolidates the accounts of all the member companies of the group. This process of consolidation involves adding together the amounts from the separate profit and loss accounts and balance sheets of each member company. Thus, turnover in a set of group accounts is the amount of turnover for each member company added together, the figure for fixed assets is the amount for fixed assets in the accounts of the parent and each subsidiary added together, and so on.

The intention is to present the picture as though there were a single big entity involved. The preparation of group accounts ignores the separate legal existence of each individual company and focuses on the existence of a single economic organisation under the control of the parent company.

Consolidation is, however, a more complex process than that simple introduction would suggest. It is not sensible to add together the separate financial statements without certain eliminations.

If the picture is to reflect the existence of a single economic organisation and the relationship of that organisation with its external economic environment, the item *shares in group undertakings* does not make sense, as it is internal to the group.

In the process of consolidation, neither the parent's investment in the subsidiary nor the amount of the subsidiary's share capital which is owned by the parent will appear in the group balance sheet. These two items are cancelled against each other.

A difficulty arises when the parent does not own all of the shares of the subsidiary. The approach in the preparation of group accounts is to consolidate *all* of the assets (and *all* of the liabilities) of the subsidiary (since all of these assets are controlled by the parent). But to balance the picture, we must recognise what is called a *minority interest*. This is the interest of the subsidiary's shareholders who are not the parent company in the assets of the subsidiary. This minority interest appears in the group balance sheet immediately after the total for *capital and reserves*. A simple illustration of what is involved appears below.

Figure 11(a): Parent Company Balance Sheet

Tangible fixed assets	£10,000
Investment in subsidiary (75% of subsidiary's share capital)	6,000
Net current assets	6,000
	£22,000
Capital and reserves	£22,000

Figure 11(b): Subsidiary Company Balance Sheet

Tangible fixed assets	£5,000
Net current assets	3,000
	£8,000
Capital and reserves	£8,000

Figure 11(c): Consolidated Balance Sheet

Tangible fixed assets (*notes 1 and 2*)	£15,000
Net current assets (*note 3*)	9,000
	£24,000
Capital and reserves (*note 2*)	£22,000
Minority interest (25% of £8,000) (*note 2*)	2,000
	£24,000

Note 1: The tangible fixed assets of the group are those of the parent company (£10,000) and those of the subsidiary company (£5,000) combined.

Note 2: The asset *investment in subsidiary* (£6,000) in the parent company's balance sheet is cancelled against the *capital and reserves* (£8,000) of the subsidiary; the difference of £2,000 represents the minority interest in the shares/net assets of the subsidiary, and is shown as a separate item on the consolidated balance sheet below the capital and reserves of the group.

Note 3: The net current assets of the group are those of the parent company (£6,000) and the subsidiary company (£3,000) combined.

Chapter 7

Analysing the Information in Financial Statements

In this chapter:

❖ How can you assess a company's performance?

❖ How do accounts assess the strength of a company's financial position?

❖ What are the relationships between the profit and loss account and the balance sheet?

ASSESSING PERFORMANCE

Profit is the main indicator of company performance, as we saw in Chapter 5. Investors and other users will focus on the amount of profit, and on changes in that amount. Sometimes, however, it is difficult to judge performance on the *amount* of profit alone. For example, the company may be increasing in value due to increased investment. The now bigger company ought to have bigger profits. Part of an increase in profit may be due simply to the increase in size of the business. To put it another way, if investors have put more resources into a company, they have a right to *expect* an increase in profits.

Also, in comparing a big company with a small company, it is necessary to recognise that the larger company should be making a larger amount of profit. To allow for differences in size, analysts and other users therefore often look at the relationship between the size of the profit and the size of the capital invested. There are various ways in which this can be done.

Return on Capital Employed (ROCE)

Perhaps the most common is to look at the *return on capital employed* (ROCE). The ROCE is a ratio that compares the overall profit to the capital or resources used in the business. This ratio will be of interest to most users.

From the profit and loss account in Chapter 5 we select the *profit before interest and taxation.* This is the top figure in the ratio. From the balance sheet in Chapter 6 we select the figure for *total assets less current liabilities* to use as the total capital employed. This is the bottom figure in the ratio. To calculate the ROCE divide the profit by the capital and then multiply by 100 to get a percentage figure.

ROCE = $\dfrac{\text{Profit before interest and taxation}}{\text{Total capital employed}} \times 100$

ROCE = $\dfrac{£3,855,000}{£21,282,000} \times 100 = 18.1\%$

The result is a return of 18.1 per cent, which gives a good basis for comparison with other companies or the same company over time. (There are many possible variations on this calculation; for instance, many analysts would deduct from total assets less current liabilities the amount of *provisions for liabilities and charges*. Also, adjustments are sometimes made to remove the profits and financial assets arising from outside investments, in order to focus on the company's central business.)

The return on capital employed will often vary from industry to industry. The riskier the business, the higher the return should be to compensate for the possibility of loss.

The return will be affected by the state of the economy. It may also be affected by the accounting methods used by the company. For example, if a company revalues its fixed assets, this will have the result of increasing its capital employed. This will reduce the percentage return. Also, whether or not goodwill is treated as an asset will have a significant effect on the calculated rate of return.

The ROCE is a reflection of two aspects of the company's business:

- The level of activity generated from its resources

- The profitability of the business.

These aspects are discussed below under *asset turnover* and *the profit margin*.

Return on Shareholders' Funds (ROSF)

Another common relationship examined is that between the profit available to investors and the resources they have provided. This is referred to as the *return on shareholders' funds* (ROSF) or the *return on shareholders' equity*.

From the profit and loss account in Chapter 5 we select the *profit for the financial year*. This is the top figure in the ratio. From the balance sheet in Chapter 6 we select the total of *capital and reserves*. This is the bottom figure in the ratio. To calculate the ROSF, divide the profit by the capital and then multiply by 100 to get a percentage figure.

$$\text{ROSF} = \frac{\text{Profit for the financial year}}{\text{Shareholders' funds}} \times 100$$

$$\text{ROSF} = \frac{£2,740,000}{£15,625,000} \times 100 = 17.5\%$$

Again, the resulting figure of 17.5 per cent is a good basis for comparison.

Asset Turnover

A measure of the activity generated can be calculated by taking the turnover or sales as a multiple of the capital employed. This is often called the *asset turnover*. The higher this multiple is, the more business activity has been created from the resources used by the company. To calculate the asset turnover, take the turnover figure from the profit and loss account and divide it by the capital employed. The capital employed is the figure for *total assets less current liabilities* from the balance sheet in Chapter 6.

Asset Turnover = $\dfrac{\text{Sales}}{\text{Capital employed}}$

Asset Turnover = $\dfrac{£18,325,000}{£21,282,000}$ = 0.86

The Profit Margin

Another measure of the profitability of the business can be calculated by taking profit as a percentage of sales, often called the *profit margin*. Take the *profit before interest and taxation* from the profit and loss account and divide by the *turnover* from the same account. Then multiply by 100.

Profit margin = $\dfrac{\text{Profit before interest and taxation}}{\text{Sales}} \times 100$

Profit margin = $\dfrac{£3,855,000}{£18,325,000} \times 100$ = 21.0%

The return on capital employed (ROCE) can now be seen to depend on two factors, the profit margin and the asset turnover. The ROCE is the profit margin multiplied by the asset turnover. (From our examples, 21.0% × 0.86 = 18.1%.) The two factors will vary from business to business. Some businesses, such as supermarkets, will have a high turnover and a low profit margin. Others may have low turnover but high profit margins.

The Gross Profit Margin and Costs

When profit margins vary (either from one company to another or from one year to the next), analysts or other users will look for an explanation. This usually leads to an examination of costs.

The *gross profit margin* is the relationship between gross profit and sales. We divide the gross profit by the revenue and multiply by 100.

Gross profit margin = $\dfrac{\text{Gross Profit}}{\text{Revenue}} \times 100$

Gross profit margin = $\dfrac{£5,456,000}{£18,325,000} \times 100 = 29.8\%$

The flip side of the gross profit margin is the cost of sales as a percentage of revenue. In our example, cost of sales amounts to 70.2 per cent of turnover. This may be compared to the previous year for the same company or to other companies in the same industry.

We can also calculate distribution costs and administrative expenses as a percentage of sales. In our example, distribution costs are 2.9 per cent of sales, and administrative expenses 6.2 per cent. The proportion of turnover accounted for by different costs and expenses will vary from industry to industry.

Other classifications of costs may be important in judging what has been happening in a company. In particular, users may be interested in seeing how much the wages and salaries paid to employees has varied as a percentage of sales since the previous year. This then might be compared to changes in some measure of the productivity of labour, such as turnover per employee.

ASSESSING FINANCIAL POSITION

Often investors and other users need to assess not just the performance but also the financial position of the company. It is no good investing in a company with high returns if those returns don't continue because the company goes out of business. Various ratios are used to assess the strength and stability of a company's financial position. As with performance ratios, these can be used to evaluate changes from year to year and for comparisons between companies.

The Current Ratio

A common ratio used in this way is the *current ratio*. The current ratio compares current assets and current liabilities. This relationship is almost always expressed by showing how many times bigger current assets are than current liabilities. This ratio shows how safe the company is by comparing assets that are likely to become cash in the next year to liabilities that will have to be paid in cash within the same period. In our example, we select the figure for current assets from the balance sheet and the figure for current liabilities (*creditors: amounts falling due within one year*). This results in the following calculation:

$$\text{Current ratio} = \frac{\text{Current assets}}{\text{Current liabilities}} = \frac{£12,833,000}{£6,237,000} = 2.06:1$$

This says that the ratio of current assets to current liabilities is a little more than 2 to 1. There are more than two pounds in current assets for every one pound in liabilities.

As might be expected, the "normal" ratio will vary from industry to industry. Manufacturing and engineering businesses will generally have higher ratios; supermarkets and service industries generally lower ratios.

The Quick Ratio

A similar ratio is often calculated by removing the figure for stocks from the current assets, on the ground that stock is slower to turn into cash. The result is referred as the *quick ratio* or the *acid test ratio*.

$$\text{Quick ratio} = \frac{\text{Current assets minus stocks}}{\text{Current liabilities}} = \frac{£7,053,000}{£6,237,000} = 1.13:1$$

Companies whose current ratio is around 2:1 might be expected to have a quick ratio in the region of 1:1. In industries where lower current ratios are expected, quick ratios may be well below 1:1. As in all of the cases that we discuss, comparison from one period to the next and comparison between companies is more important than any particular ratio.

If the calculation of the current ratio or quick ratio shows a change, or a significant difference from other companies, analysts may look for explanations.

Stock Turnover and Trade Debtors

Stocks can be compared to the cost of sales. This is expressed as *stock turnover* or the number of days' supply of stocks held by the company at the end of the year. The higher the number of days, the less efficient the company is being in getting its stocks sold to its customers.

Similarly, the trade debtors in the balance sheet may be compared to the sales or turnover figure in the profit and loss account (ideally, this would be the figure for sales on credit only, leaving out sales for immediate cash, but usually this figure is not available). The larger the amount of trade debtors in comparison to sales, the longer the number of days before cash is received from customers. The larger the figure, the less effective the company management is in this area.

The Gearing Ratio

The longer-term financial stability of a company (particularly from the point of view of an investor) may be assessed by looking at what is called its *gearing ratio*.

The gearing ratio is the relationship between debt capital (funds borrowed from banks or other lenders) and equity capital (funds supplied by shareholders). The relationship is significant because debt capital creates a legal obligation to make interest payments and to repay capital on the agreed dates. There are no such obligations in relation to share capital. Paying dividends is not a legal obligation, and only in very rare cases are shares required to be redeemed by a repayment. The higher the gearing ratio, the more risky the strategy.

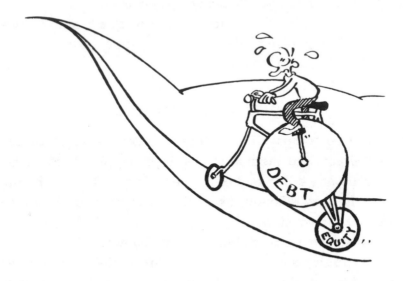

A gearing ratio is calculated by comparing debt capital to the total of debt and equity capital. In our example, we take debt capital from the balance sheet as £4,470,000 (*creditors: amounts falling due after more than one year*) plus £317,000 (the total of debenture loans and bank loans and overdrafts from *creditors: amounts falling due within one year*) and equity capital as £16,710,000 (the figure for capital and reserves and the minority interest). This leads to the calculation:

$$\text{Gearing ratio (1)} = \frac{\text{Debt capital}}{\text{Debt capital + equity capital}} \times 100$$

$$\text{Gearing ratio (1)} = \frac{\underline{£4,787,000}}{£21,497,000} \times 100 = 22.3\%$$

The same information may be conveyed in an alternative gearing ratio, which compares debt capital directly to equity capital:

Gearing ratio (2) = <u>Debt capital</u> × 100
$\qquad\qquad\qquad$ Equity capital

Gearing ratio (2) = <u>£4,787,000</u> × 100 = 28.6%
$\qquad\qquad\qquad$ £16,710,000

Either method is acceptable, but it is important that all the figures have been calculated in the same way when making comparisons.

Typical gearing ratios will vary from industry to industry and
according to the degree of risk different groups of directors are
prepared to take by borrowing. As usual, looking at ratios from
one year to the next or between companies in the same industry may identify those companies that are out of line or moving
in dangerous directions.

Another way of calculating gearing is to look at the profit and
loss account. Here, we can measure how much profit is available to cover the amount of interest to be paid. This ratio is referred to as the *interest cover*. In our example, it is calculated as
follows:

Interest cover = <u>Profit before interest payable</u>
$\qquad\qquad\qquad\quad$ Interest payable

Interest cover = <u>£3,855,000</u> = 8.17
$\qquad\qquad\qquad\quad$ £472,000

The higher the result, the safer the company is. (By contrast, a
high gearing ratio calculated by reference to the balance sheet
shows a higher risk for the stability of the company.)

CONCLUSION

This brief chapter has introduced some of the major ratios that are traditionally used in the analysis of company financial statements. There are many variations in the way these ratios are calculated. Those using them need to remember that the company's accounting methods may affect the results.

Also, ratios can be properly interpreted only by reference to the broader underlying economic circumstances. Hotel companies, for instance, *should* be showing improved profits if the tourist industry is doing very well. Interest cover *should* increase when interest rates are lower than in previous years. The effect of recent developments within the company must also be considered. For example, it may take time before it is possible to use significant new resources to make profits.

Chapter 8

Additional Information in Annual Reports

The profit and loss account provides vital information for the user about the company's financial performance for one period. The balance sheet provides equally important information about its financial position.

In addition, there are a number of other sources of useful information about a company's activities in the annual reports. Not all of these will always be included. They will often be left out when companies are not quoted on the Stock Exchange.

CASH FLOW STATEMENTS

Since 1991 companies have been required to publish an annual
cash flow statement, covering the same period as the profit and
loss account. As the title suggests, this statement shows the
flows of cash into and out of a company (or group), employing a
set of standard headings laid down by the regulations. An illustration is provided below.

Figure 12: Cash Flow Statement

	£000s	£000s
Net cash inflow from operating activities		4,234
Returns on investments and servicing of finance		
Dividends received	78	
Interest paid	(450)	
		(372)
Taxation		(427)
Capital expenditure and financial investment		
Purchase of tangible fixed assets	(2,150)	
Sale of tangible fixed assets	256	
Purchase of investment	(150)	
		(2,044)
		1,391
Equity dividends paid		(1,357)
		34
Management of liquid resources		
Purchase of government securities		(1,500)
Financing		
Proceeds of share issue	782	
Increase in bank loans	1,250	
		2,032
Increase in cash		566

The statement begins with the company's *cash flow from operating activities* (usually a cash inflow). This is closely linked with the profit figure. However, there are important reasons why the results portrayed in the profit and loss account may not correspond to performance in cash flow terms. A company reporting a strong profit performance may have a relatively poor cash inflow from operating activities, and vice versa. The explanation lies in the way in which accountants use transactions other than cash inflows and outflows to measure profit. For example:

- Sales are recognised in the profit and loss account when the goods or services are delivered to the customer. This gives a better measure of performance. However, if the company has been over-generous in the credit terms given to customers, or if customers are exceptionally slow to pay, then a high sales figure will not be matched by a corresponding cash inflow, the difference being taken up in an increase in trade debtors.

- If, just before the end of the financial year, extra stocks are purchased for cash, this will have no effect on the profit figure. So long as the stocks are unsold, they remain in the balance sheet as an asset. Only when they are sold, and become cost of sales, do they appear in the profit and loss account. However, the net amount of cash generated by operating activities will be reduced by this additional outlay.

- If pressure from suppliers to reduce the amount owed by a company forces it to make more payments to them than the amount of new purchases in the same period, then the amount of trade creditors and cash will both be reduced.

If we see the calculation of cash flow from operating activities as starting from the profit figure, and then making whatever adjustments are necessary to arrive at the associated cash flow, the three items described above represent subtractions. If trade debtors and stocks are reduced, or trade creditors allowed to increase, the adjustments will be additions. This means that the underlying cash flow is higher than the profit figure might have suggested.

Other adjustments will be necessary, the most common being in relation to depreciation. As already discussed, the charge for depreciation represents an attempt to spread the cost of a fixed asset over its useful life.

> *A company recognises a cost in using fixed assets in the profit and loss account, and deducts the amount from the original cost of the fixed asset in the balance sheet. No cash flow is involved. The cash flow took place at whatever time in the past the fixed asset was paid for. Accordingly, if the company is trying to move from the profit figure to the underlying cash flow, it must add back the amount of depreciation.*

Returns on investments and servicing of finance are used to show the cash returns generated by investments and the amount of interest paid. This may also include the amount of dividends paid on so-called preference shares, which carry a fixed rate of dividend.

After this, the cash flow in relation to *taxation* is shown. This is the tax related to the company profits and gains, and doesn't include the PAYE collected from employees (that is part of the flow from operating activities), VAT, etc.

Capital expenditure and financial investment is a very important section of the cash flow statement. It includes cash payments for fixed assets such as land and buildings and plant and machinery. It also includes cash payments for the purchase of shares and making loans. Cash receipts of the same type also come under this heading. This might include the cash received when fixed assets are sold. It will also include cash received when loans are repaid and investments sold. Excluded from this section are the cash consequences of *acquisitions and disposals*.

Acquisitions and disposals covers cash payments and receipts in relation to subsidiaries, associates and joint ventures. Joint ventures are quite similar to associates. They typically involve, say, four companies coming together to establish a fifth company. Each of the original four owns 25 per cent of the shares and the four together therefore jointly control the fifth. This heading is not included in the illustration; neither is a related heading for *dividends from joint ventures and associates*.

Equity dividends paid (dividends paid on the ordinary shares of the company, not those paid on the preference shares) are then deducted. These are considered at a relatively late stage of the cash flow statement because of their discretionary nature.

The next section deals with *management of liquid resources.* Liquid resources include cash and short-term investments that can be quickly sold. A company must manage changes in its short-term resources as efficiently as possible to ensure the best return to the company. For example, a company raises a large amount of cash for expansion. It doesn't need to use it all immediately. Its accountants purchase government securities. When the cash is needed for capital investment, the government securities can be sold. Management of liquid resources includes any inflows and outflows arising from this kind of transaction.

LIQUID ASSETS

The next section deals with *financing*. Companies frequently need funds for expansion. They raise cash by selling new shares or borrowing money. These cash inflows are called *financing* inflows. There may also be outflows, as when loans have to be repaid. Occasionally there may be an outflow in relation to share capital. This happens when the company buys back preference shares in accordance with the terms of their issue.

The net result of all of these cash transactions will explain the increase or decrease in cash during the period under review. This is the final figure in the central part of the cash flow statement. The regulations also require supporting notes, for example:

- Explaining the difference between the profit figure and the cash flow from operating activities.

- Showing the changes in the net debt of the company; that is, the difference between its total borrowings and its cash and liquid resources.

STATEMENT OF TOTAL RECOGNISED GAINS AND LOSSES

Certain gains and losses are not included in the profit and loss account. This is because they aren't closely enough related to the ordinary performance of the company. To give users the widest overall picture of the firm's performance, these gains and losses are included in this statement.

The following two examples together account for the vast majority of the items in this statement (apart from the profit as calculated in the profit and loss account, which is obviously the most important element of *total gains*).

- Increases coming from the revaluation of assets, most commonly land and buildings.

- The profit or loss arising on the conversion of the financial statements of subsidiary companies that operate in a different currency. For instance, if an Irish company has two subsidiaries, one each in Britain and in the United States, differences will arise because of exchange rate changes (which have nothing to do with the trading performance of the individual company). These changes will cause assets and liabilities to be converted at different rates at the beginning than at the end of the year.

By including these gains or losses in this statement, we prevent them from distorting the company's measured performance.

NOTES ON ACCOUNTING POLICIES

Companies have choices when certain figures are calculated. The depreciation of fixed assets, for instance, involves a choice between straight-line depreciation and the reducing balance method. In addition, the length of the useful life of the asset must be chosen.

Notes on accounting policies are used to explain to the readers both the accounting methods that have been chosen and the judgements that have been made on matters such as the useful lives of fixed assets.

NOTES TO THE FINANCIAL STATEMENTS

Details of the accounting policies may be presented before the major financial statements like the profit and loss account and the balance sheet, or after them. When they appear after them, they are often presented as the first of the notes to the financial statements. Most of these notes are provided to give more detail about the items that appear in the profit and loss account, balance sheet and cash flow statement.

Other notes provide additional information intended to help users interpret those statements, or otherwise inform them about significant aspects of the company's activities.

For large companies, one of the first notes typically breaks down the turnover figure into more specific categories. The turnover figure may be broken down by:

- Geographical area of production and geographical area of sales.

- Class of business (for instance, where a company sells two quite different types of product).

There is some flexibility in deciding what geographical divisions should be used. Breaking down the classes of business is also partly at the discretion of the directors.

Companies may also provide a more detailed breakdown in relation to their profits and net assets. It can be useful to compare the often radically different levels of profitability achieved in different types of business within the same company, and by companies operating in different countries within the same group. However, the law provides that where the disclosure of this breakdown would be "seriously prejudicial to the interests of the company" (for instance, where the information would be very helpful to competitors), then it need not be made.

Another area in which a significant amount of supporting information is provided is tangible fixed assets. A single figure for this appears in the balance sheet of most companies or groups. However, in the notes to the balance sheet, this figure is broken down in great detail. For each of several headings (typically, land and buildings, plant and machinery, fixtures and fittings, motor vehicles), there is:

- A breakdown between cost (or cost and valuation where some assets are included at a valuation) and accumulated depreciation;

- An analysis of how each of those figures has changed from the beginning of the financial period to the end.

For instance, the cost at the beginning of the year for each category will be followed by:

- The addition of the cost of new fixed assets purchased;

- The deduction of the cost of fixed assets sold;

- An adjustment to cost reflecting the change in the exchange rate used to calculate the amount of fixed assets held by overseas subsidiaries.

All of these will be added up to give the cost of each category of fixed assets at the end of the year.

Some examples of disclosure in the notes which are not linked directly to a figure in the profit and loss account or balance sheet are *particulars of staff* and *pensions.*

The total cost of paying staff may be included in the profit and loss account under the headings for *cost of sales, distribution costs* and *administrative expenses.* Even so, there is a legal requirement to provide a summary of some key employment statistics in the notes to the financial statements. The *particulars of staff* which must be given include the average number of persons employed, divided into categories. (The categories are chosen by the directors and are supposed to reflect the way in which the company is organised.) The following information must be given for each category:

• Wages and salaries

• Social welfare costs

• Other pension costs.

Information must also be given about the pension schemes operated by the company. As in many other cases of disclosure, there are limited requirements contained in the companies legislation, supplemented by more detailed disclosure requirements in professional accounting rules.

The limited legal requirements regarding pensions cover the nature of the scheme (whether defined benefit or defined contribution). The note must also say whether the scheme is externally funded or internally financed, and whether an actuary has been involved in assessing the pension costs and liabilities.

There are other areas where useful information is included in the notes to the financial statements.

The amount of interest paid must be disclosed. This is important in understanding one of the ways a business can find itself under financial pressure. At times of high interest rates, a business that has raised the finance it needs from loans, rather than through selling ordinary shares, will find its survival under threat.

Depreciation must also be disclosed. Since there is so much judgement involved in estimating this charge, it makes sense that users should be told exactly how much has been included in the financial statements for this expense.

Director's Emoluments

Certain information must be given in relation to the emoluments paid to the directors of the company. The disclosure requirements are simple: there must be shown in aggregate:

- The amount paid to directors for their services as such (that is, the fees paid to them for attending board meetings).

- The amount of other emoluments paid to directors. Many of the directors will be *executive directors* who carry out day-to-day management duties in the company. This category will cover salaries such as those paid to the *managing director, the marketing director, the finance director* and *the production director.*

- Pensions paid to directors and past directors.

- Any compensation paid to directors for loss of office.

The disclosure of directors' emoluments is a topical issue in this country. The aggregate figures don't contain specific information about compensation of individual directors.

Dissatisfaction with present levels of disclosure has been expressed by trade unionists and has been aggravated by the fact that requirements in Britain were made very much more extensive more than two decades ago. There has been no real move to follow the British lead here, although the possibility is raised every so often. Britain introduced requirements for the disclosure of the emoluments of the company chairman and of the highest paid director, if he or she received more than the chairman. In addition, the number of directors receiving emoluments within each band of £5,000 must be disclosed.

Auditors' Fees

In addition to the disclosure of the aggregate compensation of directors, the profit and loss account must also include disclosure of the compensation of the auditors.

Given that technically the auditors are legally appointed by the shareholders to examine the financial statements prepared by the directors and to report back to the shareholders, this is reasonable. In practice, however, it is the directors who decide who the auditors will be and what they should be paid. It is dif-

ficult in the vast majority of cases to see the role of the shareholders as anything more than a rubber stamp.

The underlying legal position is, nevertheless, important.
There have been a few occasions when shareholders have ignored the advice of directors who had a dispute with the auditors and wished to replace them. This effectively endorsed the
role the auditors had played in standing up to the directors to
ensure that the financial statements were fair.

VALUE ADDED STATEMENT

Companies are not obliged to include the *value added statement* in their annual reports. This kind of financial statement is
less popular than it was a few years ago. From an employee/
trade union perspective, this is unfortunate. This statement
more closely reflects the partnership perspective on the industrial or commercial enterprise. The profit and loss account is, on
the other hand, presented very much from the viewpoint of the
shareholder.

The value added statement, as its name suggests, reports on
the value added by the enterprise's activities over the past
year. This is the difference between the revenues and the *external* costs incurred.

There are obviously similarities with the profit and loss account. The key difference is that the amount paid to employees
as wages and salaries is not an *external* cost and is not deducted in arriving at the value added.

The statement then shows how value added is divided up
among the different interest groups which make up the reporting enterprise.

- Some of the value added goes to the employees as wages
  and salaries.

- Some goes to the providers of capital in the form of interest
  and dividends.

- Some is retained within the enterprise to finance future expansion (this amount is also of course owned by the shareholders).

It can be very instructive for workers to monitor the trends in these figures over a period of time. These figures give, at the firm level, the same sort of information that is given at the national level about the distribution of the national income between wages and profits.

The illustration below shows a typical value added statement. It is based on the profit and loss account in Chapter 5, and is explained below.

Figure 13: Value Added Statement

	£000s	*£000s*
Turnover		18,325
Bought-in goods and services		(9,360)
		8,965
Other income		78
Value added		9,043
Used as follows:		
Employees		4,354
Government		
Taxation		463
Providers of capital		
Interest	472	
Dividends	1,391	
		1,863
Reinvestment in the business		
Depreciation	834	
Retained profits including minority interest	1,529	
		2,363
		9,043

From the *turnover* (the same figure as in the profit and loss account), the cost of *bought-in goods and services* is deducted.

These bought-in goods and services include materials used in manufacturing, goods bought for resale, electricity and rent. Payments to employees are *not* included.

The addition of other income gives the total amount of *value added*, the wealth created by those working within the business.

The second part of the statement shows how that wealth is divided up. Employees received the largest portion, just under 50 per cent of the total (in practice, the percentage will vary from business to business). Some goes to government in the form of taxation. Some goes to the providers of capital, part as interest to banks and other lenders, part as dividends to shareholders. The rest of the value added is kept back within the business. This value also belongs to the shareholders. It can be reinvested to expand operations, and allow the creation of more value added in the future.

If you return to the labour theory of profit in Chapter 2, you can see that a value added statement goes some way towards putting numbers to the categories discussed there.

FIVE- AND TEN-YEAR SUMMARIES

Summaries of information over a period of time are often useful. Naturally, this usefulness extends to summaries of the profit and loss account and balance sheet information. Companies often produce such summaries, ignoring the detailed make-up of the figures but providing the key numbers reflecting performance and financial position over a number of years. Where there have been any changes in the way in which these figures have been calculated, figures from previous years must be altered in order to ensure comparability.

OPERATING AND FINANCIAL REVIEW

Accounting recommendations encourage companies quoted on the stock market to produce an *operating and financial review*.

This is a summary explaining to readers the policies and activities of the enterprise.

DIRECTORS' REPORT

It is a legal requirement for all companies to produce a *directors' report* to accompany the annual financial statements. This often contains brief references to the company's trading activities (by law, the report must contain "a fair review of the development of the business of the company and its subsidiaries") and details of the dividends. It must also give information on a number of other matters, including:

- The subsidiaries and associates of the company

- Details of research and development

- The existence of branches outside the State

- For certain companies, details of the major shareholders.

Directors' reports are usually brief and give little information in addition to the minimum requirements demanded by the law.

CHAIRPERSON'S STATEMENT

Companies often include in their annual reports a document under some title such as *chairperson's statement*.

This gives a more informal, and often a more public-relations-oriented view of the company's activities. A review of how well individual geographic or product-based segments of the company have performed is typically presented against a background of the overall business environment of each unit. Predictions may be made about the future economic environment, for instance, changes in consumer spending for a retail company, changes in building activity for a building materials business, changes in exchange rates for a company highly reliant on imports or exports. Changes in progress or planned for the future (new products to be launched, activities to be closed or scaled down, new acquisitions to be made in the near future, factories in the course of construction, etc.) will be discussed.

The chairman's statement will often be the most accessible information in the annual report. Research has shown that it is the part of the annual reporting package most read by the average shareholder. There is some element of risk in relying on the statement, as it is not subject to the same independent scrutiny as the financial statements themselves.

In practice, auditors review the statement to ensure that it does not contain any claims that are inconsistent with the figures in the profit and loss account and the balance sheet. Also, it would be foolish of a chairman to quote figures that could be refuted by comparison with audited figures available in the same document. However, this does not prevent chairmen from choosing to emphasise whatever information presents their company's performance (and that of themselves and their fellow directors) in the best possible light. They might, for instance, choose to focus on the profit improvement for the year, without giving adequate attention to exceptional items.

Chapter 9

What Management Wants To Know

In this chapter:

❖ **What is the role of budgets in decision making?**

❖ **Why are companies willing to spend money on budgets?**

❖ **How are budgets used to control operations?**

MANAGEMENT ACCOUNTING

The term "financial accounting" is used to describe the preparation of the profit and loss account and the balance sheet. Company accounting systems also involve preparation of internal reports to assist managers in decision-making and control. This is called *management accounting*. It includes the preparation of budgets and detailed reports on actual performance, which will be compared with the budgets.

THE BUDGET

Shareholders and others use the profit and loss account and the balance sheet to measure how well the company has performed. Management performance is judged on the basis of

what these statements show. Managers therefore devote time
and effort to predicting what the profits and financial position of
the company will be in the future. Managers are mainly concerned with making sure that profits and the financial position
are good enough to satisfy shareholders, keeping in mind the
need to satisfy other stakeholders as well. The budget is the
central element in this process for most companies.

A budget may be defined as a financial plan for the organisation. This plan is based on forecasts of the economic conditions the company will face. For instance, future wage rates
might be forecast on the basis of a national agreement. In some
expanding sectors of the economy, it could be predicted that
wage rates for new employees will rise faster than average. If
the company is importing goods from Britain or exporting its
output to the United States, managers will have to forecast the
exchange rate for sterling or the dollar. Demand for the company's products may be forecast to increase or decrease during the coming period.

Managers must also build into the budget the effect of their
own decisions. They decide on a certain selling price for their
output. They decide on the quantity of output and on employment levels. Budgets also incorporate the effects of new product developments and the purchase of new facilities.

Why Bother with Budgeting?

The time-consuming and costly process of budgeting is worthwhile for a number of reasons:

- Planning

- Co-ordination

- Communication

- Control

- Motivation

- Performance evaluation.

Planning

Without a plan, the company will have no clear direction. Ideally, the company will have a long-term strategy. The annual budget will be a detailed plan for advancing the strategic aims over the next twelve months. Even in the absence of a clear strategy, most companies find it useful to develop a specific plan for the period ahead. Unless people are forced to plan for the future, all their time may be spent on day-to-day troubleshooting. Time given to planning helps prevent a chain of similar problems arising in the future. Budgeting helps to ensure that planning time is set aside.

Co-ordination

The plans of each part of the company must be consistent. For example:

- Why is the marketing department planning to sell 200,000 units if the manufacturing department can't produce more than 150,000?

- Why plan an expansion if the skilled labour is not going to be available?

The last point shows the usefulness of planning. If a company expects an increase in demand which will outstrip the available capacity, then it is time to plan to expand capacity. Decisions must be made on building and equipping a new factory. Training programmes should be put in place to increase the supply of labour.

Communication

At the very least, the budget tells people in the organisation what is expected of them. However, it can play a much wider role in communication. In many companies, this can be achieved by involving employees in creating the budget. This kind of participation is in tune with the concept of Partnership at Work. As well as involving employees, management is kept informed of the employee viewpoint.

Control

Managers need to make sure that the company performs well and keeps up a good financial position. The budget is their plan for how this will be achieved. Proper planning, co-ordination and communication should attempt to satisfy all the different stakeholders in the enterprise. Once the budget has been agreed, it then becomes a basis (though not the only one) for management to monitor activities during the year.

- The control process works through a system of regular reporting. The company's accountants prepare a report (monthly, weekly, daily) showing what the budget was for the period, what was actually achieved, and what the difference is between the two. These differences are usually referred to as variances. These figures are often calculated on a year-to-date basis as well.

- The variances provide a basis for management to take corrective action. If sales quantities are falling below budget, management may consider what actions are necessary to eliminate the difference. If costs are excessive, they may look for alternative suppliers or seek to increase efficiency.

Budgets and the subsequent reports will be much more detailed than published profit and loss accounts and balance sheets. It is inevitable that virtually every item (there could be thousands of them) will show some variance from budget. Managers therefore focus on the most significant variances. Sometimes corrective action may not be possible:

- Forecasts about economic conditions may have been wrong

- Demand may have been lower than expected

- Exchange rates may have changed more than expected

- Labour shortages may have developed and employment costs pushed upwards.

One of the most difficult parts of using budgets to control the company is to distinguish between variances that come from poor forecasting and those that come from poor performance. Only differences that come from poor performance can lead to change in practices. Variances arising from poor forecasting can only be used to improve future forecasts.

Motivation

People respond positively to targets. A budget may therefore encourage employees and managers towards better performance. But the budget must be properly set. If a budget is set at an unrealistically high level, this will have a de-motivating effect. Employees or managers are likely to perform worse than if no budget at all had been set.

Performance Evaluation

The budget provides a basis, though not the only basis, against which the performance of individuals within the organisation can be assessed. Once more, this will depend on how realistic the budget was in the first place. Achieving a low target should not of itself entitle a manager to a bonus. Failing to meet impossible output targets should not be a basis for blaming employees.

BROADENING THE BUDGET APPROACH

When people are set targets to reach they usually try to respond. Sometimes the results can be bad for the company. If a target is set in terms of profit for a 12-month period, people may take action for this year, ignoring possible effects on profits further down the line. Some examples would be:

- Postponing maintenance on machinery to limit costs, even if the possible result is a major breakdown in the following period;

- Cancelling advertising expenditure which would not increase sales immediately but would improve sales in later years;

- Stopping training programmes which ensure qualified employees in the future.

One response to this problem is to avoid setting targets in terms of a single profit figure. Under the *balanced scorecard* approach, a range of targets is set. These focus on different aspects of the company's activities. This makes it harder for people to focus on only one aspect and damage the company's long-term prospects by ignoring all others. The balanced scorecard approach sets measures under four headings:

- Financial perspective
- Customer perspective
- Internal or quality perspective
- Innovation perspective.

The Financial Perspective

Broadening the range of measures does not require giving up the financial perspective. Profit remains an important goal. But it must be recognised that other measures, reflecting the company's overall financial position, are also important.

The Customer Perspective

Short-term profit targets are sometimes achieved at the expense of customer satisfaction. Allowing hotel rooms to become dirtier and drabber may save wages and maintenance. The guests, however, are unlikely to return. Thus, the longer-term profitability of the hotel will be damaged. Managers may guard against this by tracking customer complaints and targeting a decrease in complaints.

The Internal or Quality Perspective

Included under this heading are measures of the efficiency of various operations. Examples could include:

- The percentage of orders delivered on time

- The number of defects in a batch

- Employee turnover.

As with the customer perspective, these are non-financial measures. Sometimes they have significant advantages over financial measures.

- First, they may be easier to calculate (a simple count of employees leaving, for instance).

- Second, they may be available very quickly. The sooner information becomes available to managers, the quicker corrective action can be taken. A rise in customer complaints about the hotel rooms may lead to improvements before a serious loss of business occurs.

- Third, many managers and employees are more comfortable with non-financial information. Financial figures can sometimes be confusing and off-putting.

The Innovation Perspective

In today's rapidly changing economy, few businesses can expect to do the same thing year after year. New products, new markets, new ways of doing things become increasingly important. The fourth heading of the balanced scorecard attempts to measure how well the company and its managers are performing in this field. How many new products have appeared?

How much research and development is going on? Because of the very long-term nature of innovation efforts, clear measures are difficult to come by.

Key Performance Indicators

The *balanced scorecard* is one way of broadening the budget approach. The various measures used may also be described as *key performance indicators*. Both phrases describe an approach that links two ideas:

- Financial performance alone is an insufficient basis for control

- Long-term financial success can only be achieved if other factors are carefully watched in the short-term.

Benchmarking is another useful concept. The term *standards* describes the allowances for materials and labour used in the company's budget. The term *benchmarking* involves comparisons outside the company. The idea behind benchmarking is that a company compares its achievements with those of one or more companies in the same business. Frequently, this includes non-financial measures. Benchmark figures are sought on things like percentage defects, average time taken to respond to a customer account query, and average time between customer order and delivery.

BUDGETS: A MAGIC FORMULA?

There is a vast literature on budgets — how they operate in different companies, the effects they have on the way people behave, the ways budgets can be manipulated by managers with their own agendas, and so on. It is clear that budgets do, and probably should, operate in different ways in different organisations.

- For instance, participation in making the budget seems to work best where people have a reasonable amount of control over what they do and are not too affected by what other departments are doing. A high degree of difficulty associated with the job is also a good indicator for participation.

- Participation does not make sense where activities in one section are highly dependent on activities in another, and where the operations are very predictable and mechanised. In these areas, people seem to prefer being given a target from outside.

This suggests that a participatory approach to budgeting may work in very different ways in different organisations. There is no one formula which will apply regardless of circumstances.

Chapter 10

Environmental Reporting and Social Accounting

In this chapter:

❖ **What sort of information might be provided about environmental impacts?**

❖ **What sort of information might be provided about the social impacts of company activity?**

❖ **Why do companies often report very little about these issues?**

ENVIRONMENTAL REPORTING

Many significant aspects of a company's operations are not included in the financial statements. For instance, the future benefits created by spending money on customer relations and employee training do not appear in the balance sheet.

Another aspect of the company's operations that is not included is its impact on the environment. The operations of a chemical company, for instance, may create problems such as:

- Poor health for its employees

- Contamination of land through leaks, making it unusable for recreation or wildlife

- Air pollution, causing health problems in the general population.

In some cases, the company may be forced to bear the costs of these problems. Employees who become sick may get compensation through the courts. Often, however, companies creating environmental problems do not bear any costs. If land becomes unavailable for recreation, the cost will be borne by all the members of the community. An increase in asthma will become a cost borne by the local population in discomfort and by taxpayers in the extra cost of health services.

An environmental report would seek to offset the failure of the existing financial statements to include such costs. It would provide information to users about the environmental impact of the company. Information might be included on:

- Toxic emissions

- Compliance with environmental regulations

- Reclamation work.

There is presently no requirement on a company to include any details about its impact on the environment in its annual report. Some companies do, however, produce this kind of report. Since the reports are voluntary, it may be only those companies with a reasonable record who choose to report. Those companies that do report may provide a very biased message, emphasising the things that are favourable to their image and ignoring the things that are unfavourable.

Many believe that it is in the best interests of well-run companies to report on their environmental activities. A company considering its long-term position needs to look at the environmental impact of its activities and ensure that these are sustainable. Companies doing this might be expected to share the results with their investors and others, thereby improving their reputation. Thus, it is depressing to learn from a recent British survey that only 61 out of 350 major companies reported on environmental issues.

The position in Ireland is no better. Even where companies do decide to report, there are problems because there are no regulations governing the contents of this section of their reporting. Comparability between companies, and for one company over a number of years, may therefore be impossible. There is also a clear risk that companies will take advantage of the lack of regulations to report only what shows them in a favourable light. It is then very difficult for outsiders to distinguish between a full and honest report and one that is designed solely to present the company in a favourable light.

SOCIAL ACCOUNTING

Just as the cost of environmental damage is typically ignored in the financial statements, the social contribution of the company, both positive and negative, is usually left out.

Matters that might be covered are:

- Employment practices in general

- Policy and record on hiring people with disabilities

- Policy on hiring members of any minority community in the locality

- Employee information including gender balance in each grade

- The use of public infrastructure like roads and sewers

- Charitable contributions

- Charitable work undertaken by staff members with the encouragement of the company

- Sporting and recreational facilities provided for employees

- Availability of these facilities to the wider community

- Political contributions.

The same problems apply here as in the area of environmental accounting. There is no requirement for companies to report on all these matters. Where companies do report on some, there is the fear that they may be reporting the favourable items, and not reporting those items that would reflect badly on them. It will also be difficult to compare one company's social performance with another.

The inclusion of the environmental and social costs and benefits of a company's activities may give a very different picture of the company's role in the community. In some cases, the company's image may be enhanced. In other cases, this kind of reporting would make clear that the company needed to clean up its act.

Points to take away from Section Two

- ❖ Accounting information is useful to many different groups.

- ❖ Accounting reports are prepared mainly with the needs of shareholders in mind.

- ❖ The profit and loss account measures the performance of an enterprise for a period.

- ❖ Performance is measured by matching costs against revenues.

- ❖ Some important aspects of performance may not be shown in a profit and loss account.

- ❖ The balance sheet shows the financial position of an enterprise, by giving details of its assets, liabilities and capital.

- ❖ Some important resources of an enterprise, such as the value of its workforce, are not reflected in the balance sheet.

- ❖ Annual reports contain a range of information about financial and other aspects of an enterprise.

- ❖ Managers use budgets as a key element in their planning and control activities.

- ❖ Well-managed enterprises today make use of a range of financial and non-financial measures to monitor their progress.

- ❖ Companies do not report much information on the environmental and social aspects of their activities and this is an important issue for trade unionists to take up.

SECTION THREE

BUSINESS STUDIES: STRATEGIC PLAY

A number of new ways of organising production have been introduced over the years. Before the industrial revolution, craft production dominated. Over time, the craftsperson obtained

- Deep knowledge of the materials and processes they used to make things;

- Skills in making and using tools and;

- A good understanding of the uses to which the end product would be put.

The factory system developed in the eighteenth and nineteenth centuries. Many of the innovations in the organisation of production were first introduced in the armaments industry. Interchangeable parts were first developed in the manufacturing of rifles in America, for example. Two broad organisational principles became important in all factories, and, eventually, in service as well as industrial activities:

- Specialisation, where workplaces concentrate on particular products or services:

- Division of labour, where different workers concentrate on different tasks:

In some ways, these principles have continued to apply, though not without changes. There was a division of labour, for example, up to the early twentieth century, in which owners and managers were concerned with finances and sales, and production was left to the workers. Taylorism changed this. It was the breaking up of the production process into very small steps or components. It was designed by engineers, took thinking work away from workers, and gave control of production to managers. Fordism, introducing the moving assembly line, gave control over the speed of production to managers. By the middle of the twentieth century, workers in the main engineering industries were supposed to work in relatively unskilled, repetitive jobs. Managers, advised by skilled and educated engineers, did the thinking and made the decisions.

Elements of this Taylorist production system continue to exist in many companies. However, a number of new forms of work organisation have evolved, mostly in theory but in some companies also in practice. These new forms require workers to use and develop their skills and experience. The ultimate goal of most of the changes that owners and managers introduce into their enterprises is to become more competitive.

The main questions for unions are:

- How much of the increase in competitiveness is based on a real enhancing of the jobs of workers?

- Do they make those jobs better from the point of view of the workers themselves?

- How much is the increase in competitiveness based on intensification of work — getting workers to work harder during their normal working hours?

- Are the changes in the long run interests of workers, in terms of the work they do, in terms of the strength of the company, and in terms of the money and other returns to workers?

These questions are the main concerns of Section Three.

In Section One, we made a list of the main ways in which corporations pursue profits:

1. Reduce wages

2. Increase effort

3. Increase efficiency

4. Raise quality

5. Innovate

6. Source cheaper inputs

7. Increase sales.

We will examine the different business studies topics under each of the profit-increasing strategies. Chapter 11 examines the question of wages. Chapter 12 takes up the extraction of effort at work. Chapter 13 looks at efficiency through technological and organisational change. Chapter 14 takes up the question of quality. Chapter 15 examines innovation. Chapter 16 looks at sourcing inputs. Chapter 17 deals with selling the product. Chapter 18 wraps up the section by looking at the umbrella concept of World Class Manufacturing.

Chapter 11

A Fair Day's Pay?

In this chapter:

❖ **What is the difference between low-road and high-road corporate strategies?**

❖ **How do new forms of reward schemes, like gain-sharing and profit sharing, work?**

❖ **What is the current situation regarding pensions?**

HIGH ROAD AND LOW ROAD STRATEGIES

One way of thinking about the way companies operate is in terms of very broad strategy. The choice of strategy affects many things, including the level of pay offered. Both government policy-makers and decision-makers in enterprises can choose between:

- The high road — a high wage, high productivity strategy; or
- The low road — low wage, low cost strategies.

For an enterprise, high road means being innovative:

- Constantly changing the production processes and service delivery systems;
- Developing new products and services.

It means being flexible so that if small changes are necessary they can be made quickly. It involves being dynamic, not having a fixed, repetitive system that does not change. It means responding continually to the requirements of customers, to the advances of rivals, to innovations by suppliers. The very best enterprises don't just respond; they lead the way and other enterprises respond. High-road enterprises need to be participative at all levels and in all sections and divisions.

Some — though by no means all — enterprises that lead in their industries and sectors have relatively flat organisation structures. They are firms, for example, in which anyone who wants to speak to the chief decision-maker speaks directly to him or her. Bill Gates is reportedly accessible to any Microsoft worker in the world via the Microsoft computer network.

High-road companies strive for multi-skilled, multi-function, team-based processes and systems. The skills are high-level, requiring large amounts of training and education. To operate successfully, team-based organisations must have an element of social cohesion. They are in general well paid. The wages and salaries can be high because the competitiveness and cost effectiveness are achieved through quality, design, service and innovation rather than through low cost.

Choosing to be a high-road enterprise means choosing to compete in high-end markets, staying ahead of the posse, using the best equipment, and attracting the people with the highest skills. In general these firms do not compete on the basis of price, but on the basis of quality, design and service.

The other choice is to attempt to produce at the lowest cost — the low-road strategy.

The enterprise choosing the low-road strategy primarily emphasises reduction in costs. Within this strategy, reductions in labour costs are emphasised. Holding down wages and benefits are the chief means to this end. The low-road enterprise often produces a single product or service using traditional methods of organising production. While multi-product enterprises must develop flexibility to speed up production changes, for the single-product, low-road enterprise, flexibility is less important.

The low-cost-strategy enterprise often has an exclusively adversarial system of industrial relations. Squeezing costs to make them as low as possible requires management to drive up productivity without increasing wages. Workers will inevitably resist these pressures. The skills required in such enterprises are relatively low. The production process tends to be repetitive. The enterprise is unwilling to pay for skill. There is no incentive for training. Cost-squeezing management, adversarial industrial relations, relatively low skill levels, repetitive production work, and low levels of training can be associated with high levels of discord and conflict.

High Road	Low Road
Best practice	Low cost
Innovation	Single product
Flexibility	Repetition
Dynamism	Inflexibility
Participative	Top down
Skilled	Less skilled
Flat	Hierarchical

The two choices set out above are extremes. Most of us work in situations that are somewhere between the two.

Globalisation reduces barriers to the movements of goods, services and capital between countries. Trying to compete using a low-road strategy means having to reduce costs to where they are comparable with the lowest in the world. This imposes immense pressure on management to drive down wages. Trying to compete using a high road strategy means keeping up with — and where possible exceeding — the best in the world, with all that this implies for public and private expenditure on training and education.

How can a union and its members decide what strategy to support? The low-road strategy is unlikely to be popular with workers and their unions. On the other hand, the high-road strategy can also be implemented in ways that disadvantage workers. Most of our discussion below is about high road strategies. We aim to give a balanced view and discuss the pros and cons from a worker's perspective.

New Forms of Compensation

Below we discuss new forms of work organisation which feature direct participation by workers. In this section, we will look at *forms of payment* that are evolving to "match" the changes in work practices. There are two basic approaches to pay.

- A *fixed wage approach* where employees are paid on an hourly, weekly or monthly basis;

- A *variable wage approach* where a portion of wages fluctuate according to the performance of the company and/or the employee.

A growing number of enterprises are introducing schemes that reward workers for improvements in operational performance. Developments in reward systems are taking a variety of forms. We will narrow the discussion to *gainsharing*, *PEPPER schemes* and *skill-based pay*. PEPPER schemes include *profit sharing* and *employee share ownership plans.*

Gainsharing

Gainsharing is an incentive system that rewards employees for improved performance. The amount of gain is calculated using a previously agreed formula and then shared between employees and the company. There are two major issues in developing a gainsharing plan:

- The formula

- The employee involvement structure.

Gainsharing schemes must be designed to meet the needs of the particular enterprise and even the most basic scheme involves many different elements. Therefore, it is unlikely that any two plans will be exactly alike. In this section, we will look at some common types of schemes and the issues they raise.

Gainsharing Formulas

Four of the most common off-the-shelf models are:

- The Scanlon Plan
- The Rucker Plan
- Improshare
- KPIs (Key Performance Indicators).

The Scanlon Plan

This is named after Joseph Scanlon, a former steelworker, union official and college lecturer. This plan was devised to improve productivity. Scanlon also hoped to transform the rigid hierarchy that characterised most American companies to one where workers participated in the decision-making process. From the beginning, employee participation was linked to gainsharing.

The Scanlon plan is based on *financial data*. This type of information is gathered by companies in order to prepare their annual financial statements. Box 1 explains the details of the Scanlon formula and provides an example.

Box 1: The Scanlon Plan

The Scanlon Plan *is calculated using the following formula:*

$$\text{Baseline ratio} = \frac{\text{Labour costs}}{\text{SVOP}}$$

Sales value of production (SVOP) is sales revenue adjusted for changes in the value of goods in inventory. SVOP represents the monetary value of goods produced in a particular period of time.

> ### *Example of a Scanlon Plan*
>
> *Company records for Sweeney Ltd. show the following information for 1998, which is used to calculate the baseline ratio.*
>
> | | |
> |---|---|
> | SVOP | £1,000,000 |
> | Labour costs | 400,000 |
>
> *Baseline ratio* = $\dfrac{Labour\ costs}{SVOP}$ = 0.4
>
> *The baseline ratio of 0.4 means that labour costs are 40% of SVOP. If labour costs fall below 40% of sales, the saving or gain is distributed between employees and the company.*
>
> *We now look at the SVOP and labour costs for March, 1999. First, we calculate the "allowable labour cost" for March. Then we compare the "allowable labour cost" with the "actual labour cost". If the "allowable labour cost" is greater than the "actual labour cost", there is a gain to be shared.*
>
> #### *Actual information for March, 1999*
>
> | | |
> |---|---|
> | SVOP | £100,000 |
> | Actual labour cost (March) | 38,000 |
>
> *The allowable labour cost is calculated by multiplying the "baseline ratio" by the SVOP.*
>
> $$0.4 \times 100,000 = 40,000$$
>
> *The gain is allowable labour cost minus the actual labour cost.*
>
> $$40,000 - 38,000 = 2,000$$
>
> *2,000 is the gain to be shared.*

Source: Based on an example from George T. Milkovich and Jerry M. Newman (1999), *Compensation*, Boston: Irwin McGraw Hill, pp. 313–314.

The Rucker Plan

The Rucker plan is also based on *financial data*. However, the formula includes materials and factory overheads, as well as labour costs. Therefore, the gainsharing pool is accumulated from a wider variety of savings. Box 2 shows an example of the Rucker plan.

Box 2: The Rucker Plan

The Rucker Plan *is calculated using the following formula:*

Value added = Sales – materials – factory overheads

"Value added" is the difference between sales, and the material and overheads used to make the product/provide the service. Labour transforms or adds value to materials and factory overheads making them into products or services.

$$Baseline\ ratio = \frac{Value\ added}{Labour\ costs}$$

The baseline ratio expresses the "value added" for each pound of the total wage bill.

Example of a Rucker Plan
Company records for Byrne and Co. show the following information for 1998, which is used to calculate the **baseline ratio.**

Sales	*£1,000,000*
Materials	*200,000*
Factory overheads	*200,000*
Labour costs	*400,000*

$$Baseline\ ratio = \frac{Sales - materials - factory\ overheads}{Labour\ costs}$$

$$= \frac{£1,000,000 - 200,000 - 200,000}{400,000} = 1.5$$

We can interpret this ratio as meaning that at the baseline, £1 of labour produces £1.50 of value added. If labour becomes more productive and produces more than £1.50 per £1 of labour costs, there is a gain to be shared.

Actual information for January, 1999

Turnover	*100,000*
Materials	*19,000*
Factory overheads	*20,000*
Labour costs	*38,000*

The **expected value added** *is calculated by multiplying the baseline ratio times the actual labour costs.*

$$1.5 \times 38,000 = 57,000$$

> *However, the* **actual value added** *is:*
>
> $\quad$ *Actual Value Added $=$ Sales $-$ Materials $-$ Factory overheads*
>
> $$= 100,000 - 19,000 - 20,000 = 61,000$$
>
> *The* **gain** *is actual value added minus expected value added.*
>
> $$61,000 - 57,000 = 4,000$$
>
> *4,000 is the gain to be shared.*

Improshare

The Improshare (IMproved PROductivity through SHARing) formula is based on *physical data* rather than financial data. Any improvement in productivity, measured by labour time, is the basis of contributions to the gainsharing pool.

The baseline can be established from time and motion studies conducted by engineers or gathered from company records for a base period. An example of Improshare is shown in Box 3.

Box 3: Improshare

> **Improshare** *is calculated using the following formula:*
>
> *Standard labour hours per unit*
> $$= \frac{\textit{no. of workers } \times \textit{ no. of hours per week } \times \textit{ no. of weeks}}{\textit{no. of units produced}}$$
>
> *The "standard labour hours per unit" is the number of hours worked divided by the number of units produced. This is the length of time required to produce one unit of a company's product.*
>
> **Example of Improshare**
>
> *The following information was collected from the company records of Lyden Ltd. for 1998 and used to calculate the standard labour hours per unit.*
>
> | | |
> |---|---|
> | *Number of workers* | *100* |
> | *Number of hours worked per week* | *39* |
> | *Number of weeks* | *47* |
> | *Number of units produced* | *50,000* |

Standard labour hours per unit
$$= \frac{\textit{no. of workers} \times \textit{no. of hours per week} \times \textit{no. of weeks}}{\textit{no. of units produced}}$$

$$= \frac{100 \times 39 \times 47}{50,000} = 3.67 \textit{ hours per unit}$$

We interpret this as meaning that it takes 3.67 hours to produce one unit of the company's product. In January 1999, company records show:

Number of workers	*100*
Number of hours worked per week	*39*
Number of weeks	*4*
Number of units produced	*4,400*

We will use this information to calculate the actual labour hours per unit. *If the* actual labour hours per unit *is less than the* standard labour hours per unit, *there is a gain to be shared.*

Actual labour hours per unit
$$= \frac{100 \times 39 \times 4}{4,400} = \frac{15,600}{4,400} = 3.55 \textit{ hours per unit}$$

We then need to calculate the hours saved. First we multiply the units produced times the standard labour hours per unit. We then find the actual hours needed to produce the units.

Standard labour hours to produce 4,400 units = 4,400 × 3.67 = 16,148
Actual labour hours to produce 4,400 units = 4,400 × 3.55 = 15,620

The hours saved is equal to the Standard hours minus Actual hours.
$$16,148 - 15,620 = 528$$
To calculate the gain, multiply the hours saved times the hourly wage.

Gain = Hours saved × hourly wage
$$= 528 \times £8 = £4,224$$

Key Performance Indicators (KPIs)

All the formulas discussed so far are based on improving productivity — they focus on cutting the number or the value of inputs (labour, materials and overheads) used to produce outputs (products or services).

> **Key Point: Although productivity improvements are important to maintaining a company's competitiveness, many people argue that other factors are equally important.**

The next method of implementing gainsharing is designed to include other important factors. This approach can be more complex but is finding favour with many enterprises, as the plan can be tailored to meet their individual needs. It is called *Family of Measures* or, in Ireland, *Key Performance Indicators*.

Gainsharing plans that are based on KPIs include several independent measures of performance improvement. The gains made in each individual measure are added together to determine the size of the gainsharing pool.

An enterprise may have objectives like achieving a certain level of profits or savings, a certain rate of return on investment or growth targets. However, it needs to identify the "drivers" that get the company to the objectives. They can include product quality, process quality, customer satisfaction, on-time delivery, downtime and waste. **Drivers are factors that employees can control.**

"Measures" are the quantities that the company wants to monitor in order to improve the performance of the "drivers". Measures of performance are improved by the participation of the workers in structured employee involvement activities. Table 3 shows examples of drivers and performance measures, which can be counted physically and/or financially.

The gain is calculated by comparing the most recent measure of performance of each KPI with the base year measure. This is expressed as the percentage change in the base measure and then a money value is applied to the change. The setting of the base year measure is often called "benchmarking".

Table 3: Drivers, Performance Measures and how they are counted

Drivers	Performance measures	Methods of Measurement	
		Physical	*Financial*
Product quality	Product returns	X	
	Credits issued		X
	Internal rejects	X	
Process quality	Process interruption/downtime	X	
	Average process cycle time	X	
	Scrap or waste	X	X
Customer satisfaction	On-time delivery	X	
	Retention of customers	X	
	Reorder rate	X	

In some enterprises, management might include safety and worker absenteeism as KPIs. Unions resist the inclusion of safety on the basis that worker safety and health should be ensured by safe job design, safe tools and equipment and training. Safety and health issues should be addressed through the statutory arrangements for consultations and representation. The inclusion of absenteeism simply punishes the workers who attend work.

Gainsharing based on KPIs is independent of how the enterprise is performing financially. This means that an enterprise can lose money but still operate a gainsharing scheme, producing savings and sharing the value of the savings with the workers. Gainsharing based on KPIs can be implemented in "not for profit" enterprises, particularly in the public services sector.

Comparing the Schemes

Deciding which model or scheme is "best" depends on how well it fits into the strategy of the enterprise. To explain the differences between schemes, we can look at the following issues:

- **Inclusion of variables other than labour.** Some formulas do not include materials or overheads. Therefore, savings in these areas are not captured or shared.

- **Affected by price changes.** The price received by a company for their goods and services can go up and down. Depending on the formula, price changes can positively or negatively affect the size of the gain. However, workers generally have no influence on the company's pricing decision.

- **Inclusion of measures other than productivity.** Some gainsharing formulas focus only on productivity. Other plans include measures to improve product and process quality and customer satisfaction.

- **Financial data or physical data.** "Measures" have to be counted either physically (like in counting physical rejects) or financially (as in credits issued to customers). The different formulas use different types of information. Those that rely mainly on financial data are easy to count up, as the information is available to most companies because of their accounting practices. Gainsharing schemes that rely on physical data can involve the workers in collecting the information directly from the work processes. In very many enterprises the workers already carry out monitoring and collecting information on operational performance. This can be supported with training in quantitative techniques.

- **Extensive training requirement.** Even the most basic gainsharing scheme requires training. Workers and managers need to understand the workings of the scheme. They also need to understand and discuss how they can change their performance to contribute to a "gain". An employee participation structure usually means working in problem-solving teams of different kinds. For enterprises that are not familiar with worker participation in process improvement, this adds to the training requirement. The trend in gainsharing agreements is to include a variety of measures, all of which have to be recorded and explained. Therefore, while all gainsharing schemes require training, the more complex the scheme, the greater the training requirement.

The table below compares the four types of gainsharing plans on these issues.

Table 4: Characteristics of Gainsharing Plans

Characteristics	Scanlon	Rucker	Improshare	KPIs
Inclusion of variables other than labour	no	yes	no	yes
Affected by price changes	yes	yes	no	no
Inclusion of measures other than productivity	no	no	no	yes
Financial (f) or physical (p) data	f	f	p	f/p
Extensive training requirement	no	yes	no	yes

Gainsharing Teams

Gainsharing research suggests that the scheme needs to be implemented with an employee participation structure, generally in the form of joint management–worker teams. Gainsharing requires ideas from workers and management to improve operations. These ideas have to be channelled through the department or organisation in order to make a gain. Organised and co-ordinated teams provide the structure to channel the ideas.

Gainsharing Elements and Options

The table below shows some of the elements and options of gainsharing schemes. Schemes can be complex and some of the possibilities are listed.

Table 5: Elements and Options of Gainsharing Schemes

Elements	Options
Method of introduction	• by management • by negotiations with employee representatives/trade unions
Parties who share the gains	• employees and enterprise • employees, enterprise and shareholders
Way the "gain" is shared	• 70/30 • 50/30/20
Employee participants	• all employees • all full-time employees • non-management employees • particular divisions
Distribution of gain	• same amount to each eligible employee • different amounts based on specific criteria like salary or years of seniority
Frequency of payment	• monthly • quarterly • yearly
Formula	• Scanlon plan • Rucker plan • Improshare • KPIs
Size of (annual) bonus	• small; less than 6% of wages • large; greater than 6% of wages
Type of information used	• financial data • physical data
Establishment of baseline	• through time and motion studies • average of several years' performance • first year's performance
Relationship to non-pay benefits	• unrelated • gainsharing is tied to other benefits
Team structure	• departmental teams • interdepartmental or cross-functional teams • inter-shift teams
Duration of team existence	• permanent • temporary to solve particular problems

Frequency of team meetings	• weekly
	• monthly
Team budgets	• no budget
	• limited budget
Review of scheme	• mainly by management
	• mainly by workers
	• joint union–management
Training	• to explain the details of the scheme
	• to facilitate performance improvement

Best Practices

Because of the variations in the schemes, it is difficult to identify "best practices". The following guidelines have been developed by SIPTU to inform its participation in gainsharing.

SIPTU provides advice to its representatives under the following headings:

• *The Calculation*

• *The Participant Group*

• *The Performance Period*

• *The Payment Period*

• *The Sharing Ratio*

• *Coping with Change*

• *Buyback Provisions*

• *Involvement Systems*

• *Implementation, Monitoring and Review*

• *Approval by the Employer and Employees*

• *Training*

Monitoring should examine issues which include:

• *The level of understanding of the scheme.*

• *Whether or not improvement projects are underway.*

- *The results of improvement projects.*

- *Whether the scheme is improving the overall operation of the enterprise.*

- *The level of gain or loss experienced.*

In addition to regular monitoring, SIPTU advice is to include an annual review of the operation of the scheme. The purpose of the scheme is to ensure that the most relevant measures form the basis of the scheme and to allow for any necessary and agreed adjustments to its operation to be presented for management–union discussion.

   Key points for SIPTU Representatives are as follows.

- *Ensure adequate and trained union representation exists on the joint project (gainsharing) team.*

- *Ensure that the Feasibility Study is sufficiently wide-ranging to provide the maximum relevant information.*

- *Ensure that a good and adequate communication process exists or is established.*

- *Obtain external (union) advice when examining data sources.*

- *Ensure that all models are considered before deciding which model is used in the specific situation.*

- *Ensure that benchmark positions are fixed.*

- *Ensure that monitoring provisions are adequate.*

- *Consider how best to communicate scheme details to members.*

Source: Eugene Kearney, SIPTU, November 1999

Advantages and Disadvantages of Gainsharing for Trade Union Members

Advantages:

1. Gainsharing can be applied to all settings, including the public sector and the not-for-profit sector.

2. Rewards are closely related to employees' performance, and are not influenced by outside factors such as the strength of the market, global economic conditions, etc.

Disadvantages:

1. Gainsharing concentrates on operational performance. It may not fully reward employees for improvements in the enterprise's financial performance.

2. Gainsharing does not offer employees any voting rights.

3. Employees may need to commit themselves to demanding changes in working practices.

PEPPER SCHEMES

PEPPER is a term introduced by the European Commission. It stands for **P**articipation by **E**mployed **P**ersons in **P**rofits and **E**nterprise **R**esults. There are two main types of schemes:

- Profit sharing

- Employee share ownership.

In some companies, the two schemes co-exist or overlap.

PROFIT SHARING SCHEMES

Profit sharing is an arrangement whereby employees receive some portion of a company's profit.

Profit Sharing Elements and Options

The table below attempts to identify the different elements of profit sharing schemes and optional ways of handling each element. The list of options is not complete. There are many possible variations.

Table 6: Elements and Options of Profit Sharing Schemes

Element of scheme	Options
Participants	• particular categories of employees • everyone
Method of introduction	• by management • through a consultation process • by negotiations with employee reps/trade unions
Percentage of profit shared	• management discretion • agreed formula
Distribution of profit	• same amount to each eligible employee • different amounts based on specific criteria like salary or years of seniority
Method of payment	• cash • company shares
Timing of payment	• annually • payment deferred*
Relationship to non-pay benefits	• unrelated • profit sharing outcome is tied to other benefits
Communications	• annual announcement • periodic discussions concerning the financial status of the company

Note: * Deferred payments are placed in a special fund which is invested for the benefit of the employee. In the US, this type of scheme substitutes for pensions, a practice which is not supported by Irish trade unions.

Profit Sharing: Best Practices

If a company sees profit sharing as simply an additional fringe benefit, they may not be concerned with aligning profit sharing to a participative structure. Research by Daryl D'Art suggests that the following conditions contribute to successful profit sharing schemes (*Economic Democracy and Financial Participation*, Routledge, New York, 1992).

- **Consultation:** Employees must be consulted by management in drawing up the plan and must be involved in its administration.

- **Broad coverage:** The scheme should include all employees.

- **Predetermined formula:** The cash bonus or share allocation must be distributed to employees according to a predetermined formula worked out between management and workers.

- **Additional benefit:** It must be an addition to the standard wage and fringe benefits rather than a substitute.

- **Communication:** There must be ongoing discussions between managers and workers about the details of the plan and willingness on the company's part to disclose financial information.

Advantages and Disadvantages of Profit Sharing for Trade Union Members

Advantages:

1. Unlike gainsharing, profit sharing enables workers to benefit from all of the company's financial gains, including, for instance, extra sales which may result from increased productivity.

2. If profits are distributed in the form of ordinary shares, workers acquire voting rights in key company decisions.

Disadvantages:

1. Profit sharing schemes do not apply in the public and not-for-profit sectors.

2. Profits can be negatively affected by many variables outside of workers' performance.

3. Employers may be reluctant to offer such schemes because they require the sharing of financial information.

EMPLOYEE SHARE OWNERSHIP PLAN

In the previous section, we looked at profit sharing plans, which were paid in the form of cash or company shares. In this section, we will look at a particular, tax-saving method, used by companies to allocate shares to employees.

An *employee share ownership plan* (ESOP) is a legally established method by which a company distributes shares to its employees. Such plans are usually linked to profit through an approved profit sharing scheme (APSS). An ESOP is designed to give employees a long-term, concentrated holding of shares.

There are firms that specialise in designing ESOPs for other companies. Unions have also developed expertise through their direct involvement in the introduction of ESOPs. The structure involves an APSS and an ESOT (employee share ownership trust) which is used to finance the purchase of the shares, pay for them and allocate them to eligible employees.

A "trust" is a legal entity that controls property in the interest of another party. The ESOT is run by trustees. In this case, the trustees control the block of shares for employees until the shares are allocated. The board of trustees must include employee representation. Figure 14, and the notes that follow, show the usual operation of the ESOP.

Figure 14: How an ESOP Works

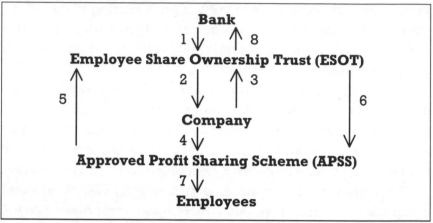

1. The ESOP begins with a loan from a financial institution, guaranteed by the company, to establish an Employee Share Ownership Trust (ESOT).

2. The trust buys a block of shares from the company.

3. Shares are transferred to the trust. The trust acts as a warehouse to hold shares in the company for the employees. During the period that the trust holds the shares, it exercises voting rights (one vote per share) in the interest of the employees.

4. The company pays money into an Approved Profit Sharing Scheme (APSS).

5. Money is transferred from the APSS to the ESOT. This, along with the dividends gained on the shares, is used to repay the loan to the bank (8).

6. Once they are paid for, a block of shares can be held in the ESOT for up to 20 years. Before they are allocated to individual employees, they must be transferred to an APSS.

7. The APSS allocates the shares to individual employees. The allocation must be made within 18 months. In order to maintain the concentration of shares in the hands of the employees, any shares sold by employees return to the trust until they are reallocated to another company employee.

ESOPs: Elements and Options

Table 7 identifies the different elements of ESOPs and the optional ways of handling each element. The options are not complete. There are many possible variations.

Table 7: Elements of ESOPs

Element of scheme	Options
Percentage of company shares to be allocated to employees	• a small percentage
	• 10% or more
Composition of trustees for ESOT	• majority employee representation
	• equal company and employee representation
	• single corporate trustee
Price of shares	• market price
	• discounted price
Purchase of shares	• paid for by company through APSS
	• cost shared between company and employees
Distribution of shares	• same amount to each employee
	• amount based on specified criteria like salary or years of seniority
Time that shares must be held	• discretion of employee
	• held until retirement or when an employee leaves the company
Length of service required for participation	• less than three years
	• three years
Communication	• annual announcement
	• periodic discussions concerning the financial status of the company
Employee representation on corporate board of directors	• yes
	• no

ESOPs: Best Practices

Different ESOPs involve different levels of employee participation. Research by Daryl D'Art (1992, op. cit.) suggests two conditions are important to employee satisfaction:

1. **Right to vote:** Employee shareholders should have a right to vote like any owners of ordinary shares.

2. **Percentage of equity:** Employee shareholders should control a significant portion of the total company shares. This portion should be at least 10 per cent.

Advantages and Disadvantages of ESOPs for Trade Union Members

Advantages:

1. Share ownership may give employees voting rights on key company decisions.

2. If stock prices rise, share ownership brings returns.

Disadvantages:

1. Share ownership plans are not available to workers in the public sector. Furthermore, due to the technical difficulties of valuing shares in companies that are not listed on the stock exchange, they may be difficult to apply in privately owned firms.

2. Many factors beyond workers' performance may affect share prices.

3. Giving out a proportion of pay in shares (even if it is in addition to the basic wage) exposes workers to risk due to share price volatility.

4. Employers may be reluctant to offer such schemes as they require the disclosure of financial information and may dilute the company's share base.

SHARE OPTION SCHEMES

Share option schemes work like this. The company sets a fixed option price for its shares and allocates a certain number of options to each eligible participant. After a specified period, participants must decide whether to exercise their options by buying shares. If the market price at the exercise date is greater than the original option price, participants can make money by exercising their options and selling the shares. The Finance Bill 2001 makes any gain from share options taxable at the low capital gains rate rather than at the higher income tax rate. Unlike APSS, not all employees are eligible to benefit from share option schemes on equal terms. Instead, 30 per cent of the allocated shares can be reserved for a select group of "key employees". The trade unions strongly opposed this aspect of the share option legislation as it is contrary to the spirit of partnership and favours the better off at the expense of the less well off.

SAVE AS YOU EARN (SAYE)

The *Save As You Earn* (SAYE) scheme came into effect in April 1999. It is similar to a scheme that was launched in the UK a few years earlier. There are two parts to the scheme:

1. Employees enter into a contractual savings scheme. They agree to save a specified amount per month, over a three-year or a five-year period; and

2. The money accumulated from the saving scheme can be used to purchase shares allocated to the employee at a fixed price under a share option scheme.

SAYE differs from the other schemes because the worker is investing his or her own income, on which s/he has paid income tax. In practice, this scheme usually complements, rather than replaces profit sharing or ESOPs. It does not require as substantial a financial commitment from employers as the other share schemes.

Advantages and Disadvantages of SAYE Schemes for Trade Union Members

Advantages:

1. If the share price falls during the savings period, workers can opt not to buy them.

2. If workers decide not to take up the share option, interest on their savings is tax-free.

3. The fixed share price can be set at a discount of up to 25 per cent of the market price at the beginning of the savings period.

Disadvantages:

1. Workers have to commit to saving a weekly or monthly amount for at least three years.

2. The interest paid on savings (even though it is tax-free) may be less than available elsewhere — this will be important if the shares fall in value.

APPROVED PROFIT SHARING SCHEMES

An *Approved Profit Sharing Scheme* (APSS) is the main employee share incentive scheme operating in the Republic of Ireland. A company must have its scheme approved by the Revenue Commissioners.

One requirement of an APSS is that all participating directors and employees must be eligible to participate on similar terms. In other words, the scheme is required by law to be inclusive.

Companies that implement an APSS receive significant tax advantages. Some of these include:

- A tax deduction for the costs of establishing and running schemes;

- Tax relief to the company for the money it diverts to profit sharing;

- Tax-free shares to employees up to certain limits if the shares are held for three years;

- Granting employees favourable tax treatment on any growth in the value of shares. If shares are sold, the capital gains tax is paid at a lower rate than income tax.

SKILL-BASED PAY

One way of determining how people who work in enterprises should be paid is on the basis of their skills. In the traditional apprenticeship system, workers received low wages during training. When they completed their apprenticeships and became journeymen, their wages increased. Thereafter wages depended on how many years of experience the journeyman had. The assumption underlying this payment system was that the more years of experience a skilled tradesman had, the more skilled he was. (There were very few women in the trades.)

In recent years, there have been significant changes to this system. First, apprenticeships are much shorter and second, employers are less interested in the traditional definitions of skills (or "trades") and more interested in people who come in with a range of basic qualifications. They are then given training in job-specific skills. The growth of the services sector and the diffusion of new technologies are speeding up this change (One reflection of the decline in trades is the growth of general workers' unions and the decline in skill-specific unions.)

It may be that the technical skills can now be obtained in much less time than they used to be, but there was a social learning process that people went through in their long apprenticeships. Pride in association with others in their trade, pride in their work, a tradition of solidarity, can all be lost through the decline of apprenticeships.

Traditional pay for specific skills still exists in some industries (such as hairdressing). However, there are now new skill-based pay systems in many enterprises, especially high-tech ones. These are systems in which pay levels are linked to the number or depth of skills an employee acquires. The aim is to provide an incentive to workers to obtain extra training or education. The upgrading of workers' skills is seen by some employers as a way of enhancing the competitiveness of the enterprise. Providing skills that are applicable across traditional trades and jobs can also be a strategy to reduce or eliminate job demarcations. Flexibility based on multi-skilling and multi-tasking can improve productivity and the operational performance of the enterprise.

A key difference in new skill-based pay systems is that the rewards are person-based rather than job-based. In the old system, all workers, say, with the same years of experience, working at the same jobs, got the same pay. In the new system any individual who acquires additional skills — for example by attending some approved course — obtains an increase in pay.

The new skill-based pay systems can be expensive to introduce. Employers are willing to incur these expenses because of the gains they expect to get from upgrading the skills and knowledge of the workforce and the increased flexibility. For these reasons, this type of system is most appropriate in enterprises where high levels of skills and knowledge are important, such as high-tech manufacturing, and modern services like some areas of banking.

While workers gain from increased wages, and from increased skills, knowledge and experience, there may also be costs to workers:

- With multi-skilling and flexibility, the employer's expectation is that workers will be more versatile. Rather than wait for others to solve problems, workers are expected to solve the problems themselves, reducing downtime. Any idle periods during the day can be filled by doing other tasks.

- Teams and work groups are expected to be less reliant on any particular individual. They are expected to have the skills to cover for any absences, at least for short periods.

- Workers must adapt more quickly to changes in technology.

- Because of multi-skilling, there may be fewer jobs. The same person or team is expected to cover production, maintenance and quality, for example.

- The minimum qualifications for entry into jobs are higher.

Key Point: As with many other innovations, the question of whether the gains for workers exceed the costs depends on the strength of the union and the complexity of the enterprises.

Only where:

- the employer is committed to continuous training and development of workers;

- the employer attaches value to the personal growth of workers;

- there are participative management practices; and

- the local union is vigilant around questions of speed-up

are the workers likely to gain on balance from skill-based pay.

On the one hand, where there is a clear commitment to workers' welfare, a skill-based pay system can encourage continual education and training, and provide rewards for increasing flexibility. On the other hand, generalising skills and eliminating traditional demarcation means workers become more interchangeable. Skill-based pay is often part of the "high road" approach to enterprise competitiveness.

PENSIONS AND OTHER BENEFITS

Pensions can be seen as part of workers' life-long earnings and/or as a social entitlement irrespective of a person's earnings during their working life. In general, socialist and social democratic political parties support the idea of pensions as a public responsibility. Conservative and liberal democratic parties generally believe pensions are the responsibility of individuals.

In most European countries there are *state pension schemes.* In Ireland, state pensions began with means-tested minimum pensions paid out of general revenues. On reaching the age of 65, people became entitled to apply for this pension. In most countries, however, the state pension alone was inadequate. People who could afford to saved during their working lives to "put by" money for their old age.

More recently, some countries have introduced compulsory, earnings-related pension schemes. This was done in order to ensure that people contributed towards their pensions. In Ireland, compulsory earnings-related pensions have not been introduced so far. This is somewhat unusual, because most other western countries, beginning with Sweden, have moved from an emphasis on minimum protection towards the provision of mandatory earnings-related pension cover. In some cases, the pension schemes were negotiated by the unions as part of national pay bargains.

Pension funds can also be run by companies for their employees, or by private financial institutions. In Ireland, trade unions negotiate the introduction of occupational pension schemes as part of the total package of rewards. The statutory framework provides for the favourable treatment of pension contributions and pension benefits. Unions like SIPTU favour the introduction of occupational schemes for all members.

In the case of people working in the public service, their contributions do not actually go into a pension fund. In Ireland they go straight into government revenues. Payment of pensions when public servants retire is made out of current government revenue. There is some discussion about the government changing this and setting aside funds specifically for future pension payments.

As with pensions, various other benefits like health insurance, crèche facilities and transport may be provided by some combination of public and private means. The extent to which they are publicly or privately funded varies from country to country, even among the members of the EU. In Ireland, there are elements of both public (state-provided) and private funding in all three of the above benefits. In some cases, employees have negotiated either the provision of these facilities by their employers, or subsidisation of the costs of the facilities.

"His entire adult lifespan is exactly eight hours.
He won't be around long enough to need benefits."

Chapter 12

A Fair Day's Work?

In this chapter:

❖ **In what ways does management attempt to increase productivity?**

❖ **When is it appropriate for workers to accept changes that increase productivity?**

❖ **What is Taylorism and does it still exist?**

❖ **How have "flexibility" and the length of the working week impacted on workers?**

SUPERVISION AND SURVEILLANCE

With the beginning of the factory system in the eighteenth century, supervision and surveillance of workers by owners and managers became possible. Up to then, most production was domestic — carried out in the worker's home. Since that time, the general view of management has been that workers should be paid for definite amounts of time, like an eight-hour day or a 35-hour week. The problem from management's perspective is that how much actual work employees do in this time is an open question.

Management can adopt different strategies to regulate work and ensure worker effort. One important strategy is supervision and surveillance (S&S).

Most business economists advising enterprises would see supervision and surveillance as justified as long as they produce results. The results they look for are increased savings and profits. They advise companies to spend on S&S as long as the last pound spent increases the companies' revenues by more than a pound. But S&S also has social and psychological costs. There is an ongoing debate about S&S.

Key Point: Some experts argue that the development of capitalism has simultaneously involved increasing control over workers.

S&S is made easier and cheaper by new technologies and new ways of organising work. Other experts disagree, arguing that the adoption of high wage strategies can lessen the need for close supervision. Either way, management has historically tried all sorts of ways to monitor workers, and workers have used all sorts of ways to avoid being monitored.

A recent innovation has been the use of computers to increase surveillance. Here are two cases of computer surveillance.

An article in the Canadian newspaper, *The Windsor Star* (10 May 1999) suggests that an extreme version of computer surveillance is being considered. This involves the implanting of microchips into workers, making it possible for detectors attached to a computer to monitor their production activity and timekeeping. There are already "smart cards" that can relay the holder's whereabouts back to a central computer, but this form of surveillance can be confused by workers swapping cards with each other every now and then. The scientist working on the implant, Professor Kevin Warwick of Reading University in England, admitted that his idea was "pushing at the limits of what society will accept". However, it is a cheap and reliable way of monitoring workers; companies with high labour costs, for which small increases in staff productivity can have a big impact on profits, are likely to find this technology particularly interesting, according to the article.

The second example involves the expanding call centre sector in Ireland. The work in call centres is highly monitored. Workers have targets. Their calls are recorded — in some cases not just the number of calls, but even the content. They are evaluated yearly and, in some companies, monthly. *The Irish Times* (24 March 2000) reported on a new software product called Acumen. It enables workers in call centres and their managers to see data on their performance on an ongoing basis. Each worker can see whether he or she is reaching the target, and management can see if the target is being reached, and if not why not.

Workers in call centres have accepted this level of surveillance because there are high rewards for achieving targets. (It should also be pointed out that in most cases these companies are not unionised.) In some companies, workers can choose what reward they want, and this makes the achievement of targets even more attractive. Use of Acumen in the telesales section of Esat Digifone (according to the company producing Acumen) increased productivity by 50 per cent.

What should union attitudes be to such intense surveillance? Where the rewards are high enough, workers are sometimes willing to accept this kind of monitoring. Generally, however, high levels of supervision and surveillance create an unpleasant and high-stress work environment. High levels of S&S may also raise civil liberties and privacy issues.

TAYLORISM, OR SCIENTIFIC MANAGEMENT

So-called Scientific Management was invented around the turn of the twentieth century by Frederick Taylor (1856–1915). Peter Drucker, the famous management "guru", has ranked Taylor as one of the most important thinkers of modern times. Efforts to give management detailed knowledge and control of what happens on the shop floor are often referred to as "Taylorism" or "neo-Taylorism" even today.

Before Taylor, how a product was produced was determined by the workers. General directives were issued by managers, but the specific production knowledge and expertise were in the hands only of the workers. Workers jealously guarded knowledge and craft skills. In some workplaces, all activity stopped when a manager was on the floor. Owners and managers were frustrated by this kind of worker's control. They were dependent on the highly skilled workers and found it hard to control the amount and pace of work.

Frederick Taylor set out to address this situation from management's point of view. Although from a wealthy family, Taylor first gained experience on the actual workplace. When he became a manager, he developed his system to transfer knowledge and control of the work process from the workers to the management.

A key feature of scientific management or Taylorism is studying the movements of workers and then subdividing the work into component parts. Each element of each task had to be separately defined. Taylor then applied his famous *time and motion studies* to each individual movement. This made it possible for management to break up skilled work into a series of unskilled tasks. Unskilled workers could be hired and told precisely what to do. Workers were to repeat the same movements, cutting out waste of time and effort. The positions of workers, machines, assembly lines and parts to be assembled, were all organised to be consistent with this principle. A detailed knowledge of each task and the time it took to do it enabled management to engage in close supervision. Taylor advocated paying bonuses to workers doing more than the average. The theory was that this management dictatorship on the shop floor would increase productivity, and hence profitability.

At the turn of the century, rather than owners (or "robber barons") controlling everything in firms, managers had more decision-making power. This was the background to the increasing adoption of Taylorist ideas. Managers' increasing decision-making power was not only at the expense of owners; it also meant less decision-making by workers. The principles of this new form of work organisation were extended beyond manufacturing to service enterprises.

Although Taylor's system was the forerunner of many of the organisational tools and technologies that exist in modern industry, there are problems with this approach:

- Taylorism required factories to work like clockwork, with clearly defined tasks, undertaken by standardised machines, methods, men and women.

- Apart from becoming tired, people also resented having to work faster than they thought safe or fair.

- People get bored doing the same, simple task all day, every day. Boredom can reduce efficiency and, at the extreme, cause unrest and disruption.

- People are now more educated when they enter the workplace. They expect to have to think more, act on their own judgement, and will often not accept simple, repetitive, unchallenging tasks.

Even Taylor himself recognised potential problems. While extolling the harmony he thought his system would bring, he nevertheless recognised that time study "may be used more or less as a club to drive the workmen into doing a larger day's work for approximately the same pay that they received in the past". (Frederick W. Taylor (1964), *Scientific Management*, Harper and Row, pp.133–4).

Taylorist principles are now in operation in pure form in very few factories in Europe. Among the aspects of modern forms of work organisation that suggest that Taylorism has been modified are:

- Built-in, rather than end-of-the-process quality control;

- Emphasis on upgrading of skills;

- Reduction of the division of labour combining job tasks and responsibilities.

Nevertheless, some experts believe that Taylorism is creeping back into the organisation of work. This can be seen particularly where work that was once high-tech is simplified — for example, computer programming. At one stage, every step in a computer program had to be written by a skilled programmer. Now there are off-the-shelf components that can be simply incorporated into programs. There is a polarisation of skills, where those designing computer packages must upgrade their skills, but those doing the simple programming and operating of the packages are required to be less skilled.

Rather than thinking about Taylorism as something that is or is not present in the way work is organised, it is better to think about how much direct control workers have over their own work. This differs between countries, between industries and between firms.

In countries like Denmark and Finland, there is a strong tradition of workers having some control and management being participative. In the USA and Britain, the tradition is much more one of routine work, well-defined jobs with clear boundaries between them and high levels of management control.

Even in recent years, while some enterprises have achieved flexibility through changes in the organisation of work, more firms have sought flexibility through flexible staffing practices, including short-term contracts for non-core employees. In Ireland, there is evidence of various levels of worker control, but the system is in general more similar to the British than the Danish employment system.

KAIZEN

Kaizen is a Japanese word meaning continuous process improvement. Continuous process improvement involves a number of steps:

- The first step is identifying the component operations that are part of the overall process;
- Then the most important operations must be identified;

- The people most directly involved are then directed to work together (often in problem-solving groups and quality focus teams) to reduce the time and resources used.

Often the emphasis is on small and incremental changes. Critics of *kaizen* have contended that this kind of worker involvement surrenders employees' intimate knowledge of the production process to management, thus completing the process begun by Frederick Taylor. *Kaizen* can be introduced in both manufacturing and service sectors. As long as there is some way of measuring what people do, it can be introduced in any sector, including the public sector.

One obvious way of increasing the speed of production and reducing the volume of resources required is to allow quality to slip. To avoid this, *kaizen* efforts usually call for changes that improve product quality as well. This is why it is often brought in with programmes like TQM (Total Quality Management). (On TQM, see Chapter 14 below.)

The pressure generated by *kaizen* can be enormous. People at all levels are required to constantly search for better ways of doing things. In the abstract, kaizening the workplace could lead to easier work, a higher quality product and a sense of empowerment on the part of employees. The practice, however, can be very different. In Japan and America, *kaizen* has most often been practised with profit as the only bottom line.

A suggestion that saves the operator from walking a few steps in the assembly of each product could save miles of travel by the end of the day. This saved time and effort, however, can be taken back by the company through assigning the worker additional tasks.

A suggestion might result in the faster delivery of parts and less downtime waiting for things to arrive. Too many such improvements, however, may result in the employee working 57 seconds out of every minute, a stated goal of some *kaizen* programmes.

In Japan, time savings are transferred to the last person on the job until that person is standing around idle for most of the day. The *kaizen* process then concentrates on ways to eliminate that person's job entirely so the whole operation can be done with fewer people.

Depending on payment systems, pressure to work more intensively can come from other workers in the team as well as from managers and supervisors. Moreover, as improvements are made, it becomes more and more difficult to find new ways of improving production (or quality), creating frustration and disappointment. In theory, it is at this point that planners, engineers or other experts are brought in to identify possible "breakthroughs". These are likely to be more radical changes than the incremental ones achieved up to that point.

Kaizen can thus involve increasing the workload of individual workers (or teams). It can also result in a reduction in the number of jobs. Alternatively, the types of contracts under which people are employed can change. The number of "permanent" jobs may be reduced and the number of "temporary" or "part-time" jobs increased. (See also below, on flexibility.)

*"You're in luck. We have two openings,
so I'm hiring you for both of them."*

Karoshi

(from "Karoshi — Death from Overwork: Occupational Health Consequences of the Japanese Production Management", by Katsuo Nishiyama and Jeffrey V. Johnson, in International Journal of Health Services, *Vol. 27, No. 4, 1997, pp. 625–641.*)

"In Japan the relationship between JPM and sudden death . . . has been an important topic of debate since the 1970s. Japanese have named these types of death karoshi, *which means 'death from overwork'.*

"Some researchers suggest that karoshi *may be typical of a new class of occupational disorders that the Japanese refer to as* gourika-byou *or 'diseases of rationalisation'. . . . The large corporations and the state have refused to compensate most victims of these disorders on the grounds that these conditions were unavoidable due to the requirements of improved productivity, or that work as a cause of these disorders has not been proved.*

> *"The combined effects of the different aspects of kaizen on karoshi is suggested by the following case study . . . In 1979, the major task of a karoshi worker (who died at the age of 45 years after 13 successive duty days, including six successive night shifts) was assembling engine parts in the model plant under the 'new producing method' at Toyo Industry Company (the new Mazda Motor Company) in Hiroshima. The line speed was two minutes per car; there was no difference in speed between shifts and no spare time, which meant this worker assembled engine parts for 250 cars every 500 minutes. The production method at Toyo involved (1) synchronised production: 'just in time', no pool of parts and no waste; (2) value organisation: to identify the spare time used by each individual worker so as to identify waste time; and (3) supplement production: to get the minimum necessary parts from suppliers and subcontractors in order to reduce stock."*

In general it is difficult to decide whether *kaizen* involves working harder or working smarter. In practice, it often implies both. As a consequence, it is difficult to adopt a single position on it from the worker's point of view. When the union is involved in the design and monitoring of *kaizen*, then the opportunity can be opened for workers to improve their experience of work and the work environment.

> **Key Point: It is essential that workers' concerns, like a decent workplace and a safe and healthy pace of work, enter into the kaizen *process bottom line.***

Making suggestions that put out a higher quality product with less strain and less wasted motion can be endorsed by everybody. Suggestions that increase the pace of work and eliminate jobs require much closer scrutiny by the union. The introduction of a *kaizen*-type programme into the workplace makes the union more important, not less.

FLEXIBILITY/SECURITY

The term flexibility is used a lot in modern business organisation theory, and particularly by business consultants. As has already been discussed under skill-based pay in Chapter 11, one way in which firms achieve flexibility is by multi-skilling. If individuals and teams have a wide range of skills, then they can handle problems that arise themselves. This involves a removal of traditional job demarcations.

Traditionally, demarcations are a part of a Taylorist organisation of work that performed a number of functions. On the one hand, they ensured that the people who undertook tasks were those who were trained for them. On the other hand, demarcations were sometimes used by workers to protect jobs that could have been open to people with less training.

The first function was important and positive from the point of view of the employer because it meant that machinery was treated properly and quality of the production process was consistent. From the point of view of the worker, demarcation was a means of ensuring the safe operation of machinery. It was also a brake on unlimited employer discretion in the assignment of jobs.

The second function of demarcation — job protection — had negative implications for employers. It increased costs over what they might have been if less trained general workers were permitted to do the work. From the point of view of the workers, demarcation prevented less trained workers from competing for their jobs and driving their wages down. It is important to recognise that if demarcation in this sense is in the interests of those in the better-paid jobs, it is against the interests of those general workers who are capable of doing the work. For unions, the challenge is to create a common identity across the entire workforce in order to build solidarity and enhance workers' bargaining power. With active union involvement, new forms of work organisation can provide the opportunity for workers to improve their pay and conditions on the basis of enhancing their skills and involvement at different levels of the enterprise.

Types of Flexibility

Functional Flexibility

The breaking down of demarcation is a part of what has come to be called functional flexibility. Functional flexibility also includes job rotation, multi-skilled work teams, and delegated responsibility. Where there are high levels of functional flexibility in firms, there should usually also be relatively high levels of skill and of training.

Numerical Flexibility

The other main kind of flexibility is numerical flexibility. This is where the numbers of people working in the enterprise can be changed quickly and easily — either up or down — in response to demand for goods or services. It therefore includes *contractual flexibility* — for example, a mix between full-time and part-time, and permanent and temporary contracts. It can also involve *flexible scheduling*, varying the amount of overtime, annualised hours and shift work.

Operational Flexibility

Sometimes the ability of the company to use sub-contracting and outsourcing is considered to be an element of numerical flexibility, but this is more usually called operational flexibility. Sub-contracting and outsourcing, like rapid changes in the number of employees, make it possible for enterprises to respond quickly to changes both in the volume of demand and in other market conditions.

Wage Flexibility

Wage flexibility allows firms to change compensation according to how well the company is doing at any given time. This usually takes the form of making part of the reward or pay package dependent on company or worker performance. Skills-related pay, performance-related pay and bonus schemes based on measured output are examples of wage flexibility. Where these are agreed, union representatives should insist that these payments be additional to good basic rates of pay.

Security and Flexibility

The security of employment is an issue closely related to flexibility, particularly numerical and operational flexibility. The very ease of hiring and firing that facilitates numerical flexibility for the employer is the cause of the insecurity for the worker.

Numerical flexibility is associated with what we earlier called low-road enterprises. Functional flexibility is associated with high-road enterprises. It is interesting to note, though, that there are elements of both (indeed all) types of flexibility in some enterprises. For example, an enterprise could have core workers that are highly (and multi-) skilled, working in teams, on permanent contracts, providing functional flexibility. At the same time, the company could also have untrained, less qualified workers, on short-term and/or part-time contracts, taken on and "let go" as dictated by short-term needs.

Research shows that advanced, functionally flexible, high road enterprises are more likely to be growing than other firms (Keith Sisson (2000), *Direct Participation and the Modernisation of Work Organisation*, Dublin: European Foundation for the Improvement of Living and Working Conditions). It follows that there is more job security in these enterprises. There are, however, two problems. The first is that most of the functionally flexible enterprises also have numerical flexibility. These workers, usually less skilled, who work under short-term and part-time contracts still have less security, even in growing enterprises. The second problem is that the research also shows that few enterprises in Europe have high functional flexibility (Sisson, 2000). So although job security may be provided by functionally flexible enterprises, there may not be enough such firms to make a difference.

Security and the State

Job security is also related to regulation by the state and by the European Union. During the 1980s and the early 1990s, some experts argued that low levels of employee protection legislation result in high employment growth. The argument is that if companies have a choice about where to set up, they will choose countries where there are few restrictions on them. Thus countries where workers' rights are most protected will be those with low employment growth. This was used to explain, for example, why the American economy has had such consistently high employment growth. There is less protection of workers by regulation there than in Europe.

The research, however, provides mixed evidence on the relationship between employment protection and levels of employment (or unemployment). Over the period of the 1980s, many European countries relaxed their rules preventing workers from being fired, wage bargaining was decentralised, and unemployment benefits were reduced. If the experts were right, this liberalisation should have resulted in lower unemployment levels, but in general it did not. At the same time, unemployment did go down in America, but inequality went up, sharply. The American system has serious downsides, which make it unsuitable as a model for Europe's future.

Ireland's recent history provides a lesson in this context. In many respects it is close to the European model. Among regulations protecting workers there are laws and regulations governing unfair dismissals, redundancy payments, and restrictions on hours worked. Since early 2000, we have minimum wage legislation. Ireland thus has a less flexible labour market than the American system. Yet in recent years it has experienced very high employment growth. (See Chapter 1 on the Celtic Tiger.) Heightened worker insecurity is not the only strategy that can be used to promote high levels of investment.

Indeed, other experts in labour relations emphasise adaptability, both on the part of workers and on the part of enterprises. They contend that adaptability to change and participation by workers in formulating and implementing firm strategy is the most important kind of flexibility in the rapidly changing world market. Workers cannot be expected to devote this kind of energy to enhancing enterprise performance if their positions are insecure. Consequently, numerical and operational flexibility can work against the implementation of other kinds of flexibility which are equally or more important.

THE WORKWEEK

Limits to the number of hours or days in the workweek are an important contractual and legal achievement by workers and their unions. The original achievement of the five-day week was not something given by the state or employers without a struggle. Workers organised in trades unions acting together in various industrial actions eventually brought the working week down from the almost impossible levels of the nineteenth century.

There are today a variety of legal restrictions on the number of hours that can be worked in a week. There is an EU-initiated 48-hour maximum. Some countries in Europe are doing better than this. France, for example, has brought in a 35-hour week since the beginning of 2000. In other countries, workweeks of 35 hours have also been agreed between employers and unions in particular industries.

The argument for shortening the workweek is both economic and social. The economic argument is that it is inefficient for some workers to work overtime while other workers are unemployed. If everyone works less in a week, all other things being equal, there will be more jobs.

One issue this raises is the distribution of skills in society. Workers with skills that are in demand are often those working long hours, while workers with redundant (or few) skills are disproportionately unemployed. This raises serious issues for the nature of society.

New technologies seem to be associated with a trend towards high levels of employment for some, and high levels of unemployment for others. This means a more unequal society. Shortening the workweek by itself cannot solve this problem. An intensive social investment in education and training is necessary to more equally distribute skills in society. Along with this kind of investment in training, a shorter workweek can contribute to lessening unemployment and inequality.

Of course, a shorter workweek is important for many other reasons. Fewer hours of work leaves employees more time to spend with their families. Community and voluntary activity would be easier to organise. People would be able to pursue education and self-development. And, not incidentally, there would be more time for just plain relaxation and leisure.

In France and elsewhere, there are mixed responses to France's newly reduced workweek. In the transport industry, some truckers (probably self-employed) objected to the 35-hour week, blockaded roads, and won concessions exempting them from the 35-hour limit. Other truckers (employees) then objected to the exemption. The IMF (International Monetary Fund) issued a statement opposing the 35-hour week in France, stating that it would not reduce unemployment and would worsen the government's budgetary problems. The ILO (International Labour Organisation), on the other hand, issued data that showed that the shorter week was associated with higher productivity. This suggests that workers make up for the fewer hours by working more effectively during the time they do work. This in turn, however, might mean that employers will not, after all, need to create additional jobs.

It is clearly too soon to arrive at definite conclusions about the impact in France. However, academic, political and trade union experts all over the world continue to support the movement for the reduction in the workweek.

SAFETY

Laws to protect the health and safety of workers, like other employee protection legislation, have been hard won. Disasters (usually fires in which large numbers of workers were killed), court cases and industrial action all contributed to the passing of occupational safety and health laws around the world. In Ireland, as with much social legislation in recent years, occupational safety and health laws follow the EU model.

The problem with occupational safety and health is that compliance is very difficult to monitor and enforce. In Ireland, the Health and Safety Authority (HSA) is responsible for developing the rules and for ensuring that they are followed. This is done through an inspectorate. Inspectors are empowered to make unannounced visits to workplaces and, if minimum precautions are not in place, to close them down. This has become more common in recent years, particularly in the construction industry, which, with agriculture, has the worst record for fatal accidents.

*"You haven't had a serious accident in 8 months,
so I know the employees could be working faster."*

The Safety, Health and Welfare at Work Act, 1989 also provides for worker involvement in safety, health and welfare. Employers are required by the obligatory written safety statement to identify hazards and assess risks in their employments. The legislation also obliges enterprises to have a "consultative mechanism" through which workers are kept informed on developments and changes. This affords them the opportunity to voice their concerns. This is strengthened by the right of workers to select Safety Representatives to represent them in discussions with management. Safety Representatives have the right to carry out inspections in the workplace to investigate accidents and complaints, and to facilities and information. Unions should and generally do provide training for members who are Safety Representatives.

The 1999 annual report of the Health and Safety Authority reported that there were 69 fatalities in Irish workplaces during the year, 18 in the Construction sector and 23 in Agriculture making these two sectors responsible for 59 per cent of the total number of fatalities. To put this in perspective: the two sectors together account for less than 20 per cent of the workforce.

Standard economic theory states that if there is higher risk of accidents — or death — in a workplace, then the pay will be higher to make up for this. What this suggests is that no protection for workers is really necessary because they are already being compensated for the higher risk. However, this assumes away the reality that once people are trained to work in, say, the construction industry, they don't really have the option to just pick up and move to a safer job. They work in the industry not because there is extra pay for the extra risk, but because that is the industry they have training for. Also, if there is unemployment, then people must take whatever job they are offered in order to support their families. They don't have to be offered extra pay to compensate for the risk of injury. They need the job, even at relatively low wages.

In the ideal world, there would be a high level of concern at all levels in the enterprise for the health and safety of workers (and, indeed, of people who live around the workplace, and who consume the products of the enterprise). In the real world, where there are pressures on enterprises to produce savings or make profits — and threats of closure if they don't — then short-term cost-cutting can often increase the risk of accidents and exposure to hazardous substances. This is why monitoring by the legal authorities is necessary.

Table 8, from the 1999 Annual Report of the HSA, shows the relatively low levels of compliance with the occupational health and safety laws among inspected workplaces.

Table 8: Level of Compliance with Health and Safety Laws

	1996	1997	1998
% Safety Statement prepared	45	48	49
% Safety Statement adequate	49	49	43
% Safety Consultation in place	46	42	41
% Safety Representative selected	16	16	17

The irony is that cutting costs by avoiding safety measures often increases costs in the long run because of the resulting injuries. This doesn't stop some firms from implementing short-term measures to cut costs that also increase the risk of accidents. It is an important function of unions to make sure that work is safe. Safe work includes a work environment, work processes, and interpersonal relations that are free of stress, bullying, and fear. A fundamental element of a fair day's work is that it should be a safe day's work.

Chapter 13

Working Smarter?

In this chapter:

❖ **How do new process, product and organisational technologies affect workers?**

❖ **What are JIT and TPM?**

❖ **What are "teams" and should unions encourage them?**

NEW TECHNOLOGIES

What is meant by "new technologies"? There are two main sources of technological change:

- *Technological changes in processes* are improvements in the machinery or other systems that produce the products or services.

- *Technological changes in products* improve the products themselves or develop new products.

Examples of process changes include the introduction of computerised monitoring and switching in the production of liquids like food or chemicals and the use of information technology in the provision of services such as in banking, the travel business and in office procedures of many different kinds. An example of new technology in products is the introduction of liquid crystal screens for computers.

A process change for one industry could be a product change for another. For example, the use of computers in both manufacturing and services is a process change. The computers themselves may be new products of the computer industry.

The key technological changes of the past few decades are those relating to the microprocessor. These have made possible the *technological convergence* between information and communication technologies (ICT). This convergence means that computers and telephones — and, eventually, televisions — will all merge into a single product. From this new product we will obtain information, analyse and organise it into easily digestible forms, and distribute it. Information here includes not just data and figures required, say, by banks and government, but also music, newspapers, films and other entertainment used by individual households. The World Wide Web (www) through which electronic commerce (e-commerce) takes place is presently the main infrastructure for ICT.

Together with new transport technologies and new ways of organising large firms, the new ICTs have contributed to the increasing internationalisation of the economy often referred to as *globalisation*. Globalisation means that most firms — even in small, peripheral countries like Ireland — are subject to competition from rival firms elsewhere in the world. Globalisation also means that most firms — in both production and services — have choices as to where they locate. Economic geographer, Professor Ann Markusen, has described this freedom of choice about location as "slippery space". How to encourage economic activity *and keep it* in Ireland is the problem of how to make Ireland a "sticky place in slippery space". (See Chapter 1 on Ireland in the global economy.)

How should workers and unions approach the new technologies? Working smarter means achieving increased output without increased effort. There is of course a blurred line between working harder and working smarter. If nothing else, there is increased effort involved in undergoing training for new technologies. This training may be an essential part of working smarter. Should workers be paid more for the job that they do following the upgrading of their skills? Should they be paid more to accept new technologies or new work practices? After all, the introduction of the new technologies, which increase productivity, savings and profits, may be impossible without their co-operation. On the other hand, globalisation sets limits to what can be accomplished. In industries where technologies are changing rapidly, an adaptive proactive response by unions has more chance of success than outright opposition to technical change. Enterprises that fail to adapt and invest in new technologies risk becoming uncompetitive, with serious negative consequences for the workers.

> **Key Point:** *There are limits to what unions can and should accept, even in globalised industries where increasing costs can result in closure. At the extreme, intensive, exploitative, low-paid, unsafe jobs could be worse than no jobs.*

NEW FORMS OF WORK ORGANISATION

New forms of work organisation are a type of new technology, often called "soft" technological change as opposed to "hard" technology, which involves machinery. Consequently, much of what was said above about new product and process technologies can also be applied to new forms of work organisation as a kind of soft technology.

The term "new forms of work organisation" refers to the introduction of various types of innovations in organisation, including:

1. Team working (and, in manufacturing in particular, cellular production);

2. Direct employee involvement in various levels of decision-making;

3. One or more of JIT, TPM, TQM, etc.

The question of the appropriate approach by unions to the introduction of new forms of work organisation is similar to that relating to the introduction of any new technology. The main difference is that new forms of work organisation can be less obvious, as changes may be introduced more gradually than "hard" technologies, like new machinery. Workers must be clear about what is involved in the various new forms of work organisation and must be able to recognise them when they are proposed or introduced. What they do about it depends on the circumstances in the particular enterprise.

How common are new forms of work organisation in Ireland? There is some disagreement about the answers to these questions. Different surveys have produced different results.

One study was done by McCartney and Teague in 1998. They found job rotation, quality circles, TQM and team working to be widespread in Ireland in selected sectors.

Another study in 1998 by Roche and Geary concluded that, in unionised workplaces,

> . . . employers in the main have continued to regulate the workplace through unilateral managerial control and collective bargaining. Workplace partnership had never been used to introduce change in more than a fifth of workplaces. In most instances, a little more than one in ten employers used it and it was rarely if ever adopted in strategic areas of management decision-making.

The national agreement "Partnership 2000", which was implemented from 1997, provided the first nationally agreed framework for the development of partnership approaches at the enterprise level. Under this type of agreement, the local practice of partnership approaches will be encouraged.

We can conclude cautiously that there is some evidence of new forms of work organisation in Ireland, and that it is growing. Roche and Geary seem convinced, however, that even in the presence of increasing globalisation and competition, most firms will avoid collaborative production, relying on "traditional exclusionary management practices" to achieve the required levels of dynamism. Whether or not this is true depends at least in part on the strategies adopted by the unions.

JUST-IN-TIME (JIT)

Just-in-Time (JIT) aims to minimise inventories on the factory floor. Many of the techniques used in JIT are based on the Toyota Production System, which was developed by Taiichi Ohno.

Ohno emphasised producing on a timely basis — what is wanted, when it is wanted, in the quantity that is wanted, no less but also no more. The idea is to make only to customer order, to exact customer requirements and to deliver when the customer wants it.

With JIT, parts and materials must be delivered by suppliers right when they are needed. Buffer stocks are not allowed to build up between workstations. Ideally, finished products are produced just when customers are ready to take delivery of them. The location of everything within the factory is carefully planned for continuous production. Work flows from one process to the next on a "just-in-time" basis. Equipment is located so as to smoothly receive its input from the previous process and smoothly pass on its output to the next stage of production. Machines that produce more than enough to meet the immediate needs of the next stage in production are redesigned. Large, dedicated machines are replaced by smaller, more flexible machines.

The proponents of JIT claim this disciplined approach sets the stage for savings in time, effort, labour, space, finance and rework. JIT is more than an inventory-reducing system. Accumulated inventories and work-in-progress hide production problems, such as scrap, downtime, poor training and defective deliveries. Reducing work-in-progress forces companies to deal with the production problems which inventories hide.

There are probably no enterprises that completely match this description of JIT. Many enterprises, however, have JIT programmes, in which the aim is to continuously work toward complete JIT.

JIT is often implemented with other new production concepts. For example, continuous production is impossible if there are constant hold-ups because of quality problems. TQM (see Chapter 14) is therefore usually brought in alongside JIT. Equipment breakdown is especially damaging in a JIT workplace. Consequently, Total Productive (Preventive) Maintenance (TPM) is often implemented at the same time.

Kanban

One JIT technique is the kanban system. Kanban is Japanese for "card". In this kind of system, cards are used as signals to pull parts into production when they are required. For instance, when an operator is finished with a bin of parts, a card is sent to stores and the bin is replaced. Stocks are never delivered unless the card comes in. Work-in-progress is considerably reduced.

Supply-chain Management

To be successful, JIT requires supply chain management. In one plant, the kanban system can reduce inventories. But a close relationship with the outside suppliers of inputs is necessary if these suppliers are to deliver just in time. And those suppliers must also have a close relationship with *their* suppliers. If there is any weakness along the supply chain, then JIT can break down. If suppliers of components get into difficulty — either with their suppliers, or with industrial relations disputes, or whatever — then the company will not receive these parts and will not be able to supply just in time.

The tightly interrelated nature of JIT production means that industrial action can be more effective. Stoppages at one point in the chain can shut down the entire production process. There are no inventories for the company to fall back on.

Flexibility

One objective of JIT programmes is to increase manufacturing flexibility. If production responds only to the immediate needs of the next workstation, the final product can be quickly changed and the necessary adjustment can cascade back through the system. When demand decreases, whole groups of workers and equipment can be taken off line without interrupting the production of the rest. Output can be expanded in the same way.

Cellular Manufacturing and Multi-skilling

"Cellular" manufacturing is usually considered essential in JIT. In a cellular layout, work is physically organised so that a group of machines and/or people complete the product or a number of products. In this sense, each cell is a separable and independent part of the production process. Operators are usually multi-skilled and the cell is flexible in terms of the quantity and type of products manufactured. The workers in the cell are usually considered as a team or part of a team. (see the section on teams below). Training workers to be multi-skilled may increase the variety in people's jobs. On the other hand, the ability to do several jobs may keep the worker running every minute of the day. The "flexible", multi-skilled, cross-trained worker may have to complete tasks like routine maintenance or general housekeeping to "mop up" any remaining idle time. In non-manufacturing enterprises, the principles of cellular and multi-skill working can be seen in the idea of the "one stop shop" responsible for a range of work tasks that are shared by the work group.

Porosity

From the point of view of workers, JIT means no waiting for work to arrive — there is no "standing around". What this implies is much more intensive work. Researchers have looked at what they call the "porosity" of the working day. The word comes from "porous", meaning having openings permeable to water. A working day with high porosity is one in which there are many breaks or changes. An example of porosity is where, instead of having to stand at her work position at all times, a worker must occasionally go to an office, or consult a supervisor in another part of the factory, or check something in a storeroom.

Given the choice, most people would prefer high porosity in their work. JIT is about the elimination of porosity.

JIT also makes it harder to vary the pace of work. The lack of inventories means it is not possible to earn a breather by temporarily working faster or falling back on accumulated stocks. When something goes wrong, there is no slack in the system. The workers on the floor are responsible for immediately correcting any problem that may interrupt the flow of work. To the extent that JIT increases productivity, it could mean fewer jobs and harder work.

Key Point: Workers and unions must be aware of both the costs and benefits of JIT when negotiating its introduction.

TOTAL PREVENTIVE MAINTENANCE (TPM)

Total preventive maintenance (TPM) involves servicing and maintaining machinery, tools, and other equipment regularly. The fundamental purpose is to make sure that whenever equipment is needed, it will be available. It also prolongs the life of the equipment. The aims of TPM (sometimes called total productive maintenance) are:

1. To ensure that any problems or potential problems in machinery are identified before there is a breakdown. The idea here is that prevention of breakdowns is cheaper than dealing with problems that arise as a result of breakdowns.

2. To transfer maintenance tasks, where appropriate, to machine operators.

The types of repetitive maintenance tasks carried out by the machine operator include cleaning, lubricating and making basic repairs. This means that the maintenance technician can spend more time on more technical tasks such as working on equipment design faults.

TPM also provides the opportunity to gather information about the equipment and the best way to keep it maintained. This information can be collected by both operators and technicians and developed into accurate maintenance procedures. Reasons for machine failure can be incorporated into these procedures and updated as required. A preventive maintenance system can also help with predicting equipment failure. If the condition of the machinery is monitored, then problems can be anticipated in advance. If an effective equipment maintenance procedure is set up, the costs of replacing parts and recovering from machine downtime are often greatly reduced.

Depending on the circumstances, TPM can have negative and/or positive implications for workers. For example, TPM can be used by management to increase the workload of machine operators by adding maintenance tasks. TPM in these circumstances is a guise under which unpaid-for increases in productivity are extracted from the workforce.

On the other hand, TPM relies on the knowledge and experience of machine operators. Through training, TPM can increase the skills and responsibility of these workers. The introduction of TPM should be accompanied by appropriate payment systems and compensating reductions in other tasks.

TEAMS

We have already discussed teams, work groups and multi-skilling a number of times in this book. Here we provide a formal definition and consider the contribution of this new form of work organisation to working smarter.

There are four main criteria that qualify work group units to be considered teams:

1. There are only a few members — from five to 20. Despite the rhetoric, management experts don't usually consider an entire workplace to be "a team".

2. Individually or together, the group has a range of complementary skills.

3. The team has a common purpose or task.

4. Each member of the team is equally responsible for achieving the common purpose.

In the recent EPOC study on teams, the title summarises the findings: *Useful but Unused — Group Work in Europe.* Based on a 1996 survey, the study concluded that "the application of group work is modest, and . . . group delegation is in its infancy in European workplaces". Although Ireland is above the European average in terms of group delegation, it is below the Netherlands and Sweden. There is a question over how much team-based production there is likely to be in future. Some consider it to be an inevitable route that advanced firms will take, others that firms will in general continue to use traditional methods.

It is generally the case that a team can work more quickly, efficiently and cheaply than a collection of isolated individuals. This is especially true when the job requires a mix of skills, co-operation, judgement and experience. For teams to operate successfully, the members have to trust one another, there must be a high level of transparency in the firm, and there must be commitment to the change on the part of senior management. Generally, new forms of payment are also required, and training is necessary both in the skills necessary to do the job and in how to function as a team.

Teams came into vogue in the 1980s. Some teams were established on the Japanese model. Others looked to teamwork that was being developed in the Swedish automobile industry. The two models are very different. The table below compares the Japanese and Swedish models of teams.

From the point of view of workers and their unions, the issues are similar to those discussed under many of the other topics in Section Three.

Teams can be used to increase worker involvement, making jobs more interesting and increasing the acquisition of skills and training. Where teamwork really is smarter work, it may be smart for unions to support it. Properly designed teamwork, with union involvement and explicit aims to improve the quality of working life, can be a better way of working than the traditional Taylorist model. Where teams are used solely to increase management discretion in the assignment of work and to increase the workload, they deserve a much more critical look.

Table 9: Japanese and Swedish Team Models Compared

	Japanese	Swedish
Production arrangement	Assembly lines with Just-in-Time control	Stationary assembly of the whole product or large components
Tasks	Highly repetitive work; one minute to complete tasks	Extensive tasks with work times of over an hour
Relation between groups or teams	Teams tightly linked through the elimination of buffers and variation in work pace	Reduction of linkages through allowing variation in work pace
Supervision	Close supervision	Reduced supervision; daily responsibility delegated to teams
Work intensity	Intense managerial pressure for maximum performance	Performance limits specified in contract between company and union
Team leader	Selected by management	Elected by team or rotated
Decision-making	Suggestions from teams; final decision by management	Independent decisions taken by teams
Union role	Work organisation, production pace and job design defined exclusively by company	Work organisation regulated by contract; union involved at all levels of management
Limits of participation	Teamwork closely tied to management perspective	Work organisation a compromise between partly opposed interests

How not to do teams . . .

A job ad from a Pittsburgh paper:
Robot Technician
Robot Technicians assist a robotic prescription-filling unit with filling prescriptions. Duties include preparing prescription vials, loading those vials onto the robot, and stocking the robot with appropriate drugs. Very fast-paced, team-oriented position that requires a lot of standing. No experience necessary.

One important lesson to be learned from overseas is that teams are no substitute for the union.

Key Point: Teamwork raises just as many, if not more, issues as traditional work organisation where workers need union organisation and representation.

Chapter 14

Pursuing Quality

In this chapter:

❖ **What are the ideas behind Total Quality Management (TQM)?**

❖ **How does Statistical Process Control (SPC) work?**

❖ **What are Quality Circles?**

❖ **Why might unions have concerns about TQM?**

The issue of quality in general arose first in the move from craft to factory production in the eighteenth and nineteenth centuries. When a product is produced by a craftsman, quality is built in. Each unit is unique. In factory production, the notion of standardised and interchangeable parts is introduced. But if the final product doesn't work, it must be scrapped. Inspection of parts to ensure quality was introduced to reduce wastage costs. Because it would be too time-consuming to inspect every part, "spot" checks were made. Statistical methods were introduced around the beginning of the twentieth century to calculate the minimum number of checks necessary to ensure a high probability of quality. Inspection of the final product ensured a quality product to the customer. Catching faulty products at this last stage, however, meant scrapped products and substantial costs.

TOTAL QUALITY MANAGEMENT

Total quality management (TQM) is an alternative to the traditional approach to quality.

Rather than spot-checking parts and final inspection, TQM aims to improve quality by involving all employees at each stage of the production process.

However, TQM is about much more than just increasing customer satisfaction. This is clear from the fact that, under TQM, ongoing improvement in quality is to be achieved by an ongoing reduction in costs. This is often expressed in terms of "value adding" and "non-value adding". TQM aims to identify and then eliminate those things in work that do not add value.

As with other new management systems, this raises important questions:

- What is the role of workers in TQM?

- To what extent should workers share in the gains or savings?

Whether or to what extent workers derive benefits from the improvements depends on the industrial relations situation and the competitive position of the enterprise.

When an enterprise is implementing TQM, the importance of work being carried out with no defects is emphasised by such phrases as "right first time". Everybody is encouraged to view the person whom they hand work on to as their "internal customer". Providing a fault-free service or product to the final customer results from providing such services or products to internal customers. This means ensuring that both paperwork — such as customer order forms — and manufactured products or sub-components of the product are not passed on until everything is correct and fault-free.

In practice, this means that quality is defined as conformance to specifications. The goal of improving quality is pursued through reducing variation. It should be noted that this type of consistency is only one aspect of what people ordinarily mean when they talk about quality. A cheaper brand-name radio might perform consistently, but models with better sound and longer lifespans would generally be regarded as having more or higher quality. TQM is about achieving consistency, not producing all-round higher quality, especially if all-round higher quality would increase costs. In service enterprises and in office-based work, TQM-type principles are sometimes introduced under the name of *process redesign*.

Statistical Process Control

One of the ways in which the reduction in variation is pursued is *statistical process control* (SPC). SPC is a data-based quality control system originally designed to suit Taylorism. Much of the original work was done in the 1920s by Walter Shewhart, who contributed hugely to what became SPC. He considered control in manufacturing to be based on:

- Specification of requirements;

- Production in accordance with that specification;

- Determination of whether the requirements are met through inspection.

Inspection, however, could never be exact. He therefore focused on how to control the variation in production. This led to the need to specify precisely the dimensions of the part or product, and also the performance of the operator.

A key distinction between the original use of statistics for quality control and SPC is that originally statistics helped in deciding how much inspection there should be. The data could show how much inspection cost, and how much it saved.

With SPC, keeping statistics is aimed at determining the variations in each operation's output. In SPC, quality comes not from more effective scrappage, but from changing the process to reduce variation and, as a result, to reduce wastage.

When the process involved is a chemical or other automated element of production, changing it could mean some strictly scientific improvement. When the process is some action or series of actions that workers do, standardisation and the reduction of variation is likely to be a much more mixed blessing:

- TQM modifies Taylorism in increasing worker's responsibility for monitoring both the inputs and outputs of the production process through the "internal customer" concept.

- TQM brings Taylorism back in through the side door by reducing the variation in workers' activities, leading to standardised work which is easy to time study and supervise.

Reducing variance usually has a cost. Work can become more monotonous. Standardised movements can lead to repetitive strain injuries. Changing a process could require an increase in workers' effort. Note that this increased effort is not necessarily physical; it could also be mental. Adjusting a process could, for example, result in less physical effort but the need for more mental alertness.

Quality Circles

TQM is closely related to other recent management innovations. Teamwork is an important part of the TQM process. Teams involving people from all areas of the organisation are often set up to try and solve particular problems. One type of teamwork in TQM was known as *quality circles*. Since the late 1980s, these have been introduced under different names. They include Task Forces, Quality Focus Groups and Quality Improvement Teams.

Though probably originating in America, this idea was first widely adopted and developed in Japan. The quality circle is really a quality improvement team, usually made up of between five and ten people, often from different levels in the organisation, who meet regularly to discuss quality-related work problems. They look at these problems and suggest solutions. To be effective, the circle must be trained in the tools of TQM, and must be empowered to promote and implement the quality improvements.

Union Concerns about TQM

- Management-determined models of TQM very often ignore the political difficulties within the firm. Management is viewed as "rational" and "speaking with one voice". In reality, the commitment by top management may not be matched in the middle, on the line or in the office.

- In TQM, quality becomes the responsibility of the direct worker, rather than the quality inspector. Is the pay of the direct operator increased in relation to this increase in responsibility?

- Each worker is governed by the "internal customer" or the next worker in the production process. This means that a fellow worker/colleague is operating a control and surveillance role. This can increase the stress inherent in work and could fracture worker solidarity.

- Reducing variation in the work process can lead to deterioration in working conditions and damage workers' health.

These possibilities highlight the need for workers to involve their union representatives in discussions with management at the earliest possible stage. Unions need to provide professional representation, information, and training to ensure that the interests of workers are fully taken into account in the design of TQM. For instance, SIPTU provides courses on TQM and work organisation as well as enterprise-specific training to workplace union representatives.

Chapter 15

Innovation

THE LEARNING ORGANISATION

The learning firm — or, more generally, the learning organisation — is an adaptable one. It is an organisation capable of changing rapidly in response to the market or other competitive pressures with new products or services. The learning organisation is also capable of bringing new approaches to existing products that results in improving quality, design and cost. It is an organisation that is constantly changing.

Learning firms must continuously upgrade the skills of managers and workers. They rely on having flat organisation structures, minimising the layers of bureaucracy between the top decision-makers and those who actually make and distribute the product or provide the service. Responsibilities are delegated downward to employees and teams. The learning organisation is likely to be a high-road enterprise.

The learning organisation encourages employees to share knowledge with others in the enterprise. The knowledge and experience of individuals working in the organisation become part of the knowledge of the enterprise. When people leave, retire or die, this does not leave major gaps in the organisation's ability to function.

Most managers of big companies in Ireland (as in Britain and America) are trained in finance and accounting. In Japan and Germany, most managers are technically trained in science or engineering. The latter have a much better understanding of manufacturing or the provision of services. Since they have more often worked their way up in the organisation, these managers are also more committed to the enterprise. Managers with this background are more likely to move their organisations in a learning direction.

While elements of the learning organisation may be present in many enterprises, very few have all the characteristics. Recent research suggests that the process of learning within firms is enhanced by the sharing of knowledge and experience between companies. In some regions in Europe, companies have achieved success by being part of a group of enterprises working closely with one another. One explanation for this is that even more learning is taking place through sharing the diverse experiences of the different organisations.

This kind of exchange requires high levels of trust among the enterprises. This is usually possible only where there are political, social and cultural commonalities, which promote communication among the owners and employees across the different enterprises.

Elements of this kind of learning region are present in parts of Ireland — particularly in the furniture industry in Monaghan — but not to the same extent as in other parts of Europe, such as Emilia Romagna in Italy. In this part of Italy, there are many villages with successful groups of companies, competing internationally in industries like ceramic tiles, clothing, textile design and footwear.

The success of these regions raises important policy questions. Can government take action to encourage the development of learning enterprises co-operating within industrial districts. Most experts believe that where the potential is already there, it can be encouraged, but where there is little or no potential in place, it cannot be artificially created.

A more limited question is whether policies can encourage individual enterprises to become learning organisations. It is clear that very few companies in Ireland are fully fledged learning enterprises. Ireland is not unusual in this respect in Europe. One reason for this is that learning enterprises need to plan for the long haul. The government and financial considerations on the contrary encourage short- to medium-term perspectives.

Significant shifts in tax legislation and bank lending policies are a necessary first move in encouraging long-term perspectives and learning enterprises.

RESEARCH AND DEVELOPMENT (R&D)

In the simple model of profits that we developed in Chapter 2 there was no mention of R&D. In reality, firms do invest in R&D in order to invent new products and improve old ones. R&D is also undertaken in search of new production processes. In industries particularly dependent on new products, like the pharmaceutical, electronics and software industries, R&D spending can be as high as 15 per cent of the revenue of the industry.

R&D changes enterprises and industries by changing their products and processes. It has the potential to increase the volume of production through increasing efficiency rather than increasing effort. Globalisation and the resultant intensification of competition has put pressure on enterprises to increase their emphasis on R&D.

NATIONAL SYSTEMS OF INNOVATION (NSI)

Technological change and innovation were traditionally seen as taking place in isolation. While the availability of venture capital was often stressed, enterprises were generally regarded as either innovative or not. Little attention was paid to the overall environment surrounding the firm.

It is now recognised that social factors can influence whether enterprises in a region or country are innovative — the quality of the education system, for example, or the creativity of employees. The level of trust between managers of similar firms determines how willing they are to share information about innovations with each other. Education, culture, inter-firm relations, employer–union relations, together with research institutions, research firms, and universities, are all part of the national system of innovation. Different industrial relations systems like the national partnership agreements can contribute to innovation. The better these elements work together, the more innovative the society and its enterprises will be. These factors also influence the start-up of new companies. Taken together, these institutions have been called the *National System of Innovation (NSI)*.

The effectiveness of the NSI can change over time. British inventions and innovations led the way for the rest of the world in the nineteenth century, but have not been so frequent or important in recent decades. America, Japan and Germany have had more successful systems of innovation in recent decades.

In some cases, a local system of innovation can be more important than the overall national system of innovation. In some localities, there may be a large number of small companies, all in one industry or even one sub-sector. These companies may employ workers with similar skills and training, workers who were born in that place and brought up knowing that industry. Each company may specialise on a small range of tasks, but all the companies together have a wide range of capabilities. This is called *flexible specialisation*. If there are also local research, education and training facilities, then this all constitutes a local system of innovation. In these locations, the rate of improvement in production methods can be very rapid.

A local system of innovation may be successful even though the national system of which it is a part is not so successful. This is the case in Italy, where the region of Emilia Romagna has been more successful — and more consistently successful — than Italy as a whole.

There is now quite a deep understanding of the reasons for the successes of Emilia Romagna, but it turns out this success is hard to generalise. The problem is that among the reasons for the success are many years of shared culture and values. The region has a tradition of artisanal associations, and many other social, political and economic institutions in which people interact. All this adds enormously to trust, and places social limits on economic freedom.

If the owner of one firm has an opportunity to take over the customers of another local business — or otherwise use a perfectly legal business practice to get the better of it — the opportunity will not be taken. It is too socially costly. If a company stepped over the line of acceptable local business practice, then other owners in the area will stop doing business with it. They will probably stop socialising with the owner as well.

The historical basis for successful local systems of innovation is difficult to create. It takes a long time. Elements of such systems can be encouraged, though. Interaction between workers and owners of different small enterprises can be promoted. Information-sharing can be encouraged and networks established. Efforts like this can provide some of the advantages of successful local systems of innovation.

The Irish government's funding of MediaLab Europe is an example of an attempt to create a local system of innovation in a particular sector, multimedia production. This approach has been criticised for being too "top-down". Unions can contribute to a more "bottom-up" approach.

> **Key Point: Since unions organise across different firms, unions are sometimes in a position to promote the sharing of experience and expertise among enterprises.**

SIPTU's Participation Network is an example of how a union can develop shared learning between union representatives from different kinds of enterprises and sectors. In Ireland, a pilot programme financially assisted the creation of networks among small and medium-sized companies. The funding was not continued, however.

Chapter 16

Sourcing Inputs

In this chapter:

❖ **Why are outsourcing and sub-contracting important?**

❖ **What should workers' attitudes be to outsourcing and sub-contracting?**

We have already introduced outsourcing in our discussion of supply chain management in Chapter 13. All organisations buy goods and services from other organisations. This is true for manufacturing and service firms in the private sector. It is also true in the public sector.

What is the difference between buying something that an enterprise needs and outsourcing?

Part of the answer to this question is whether the organisation doing the buying could, without significant change, provide the bought-in good or service itself. If the enterprise has always bought the input in from outside, however, then the buying-in would not be considered outsourcing, even if the buying organisation could potentially provide the good or service itself. Another part of the answer, then, is whether the organisation usually makes the good or provides the service itself.

Outsourcing takes many forms and can be undertaken for different reasons. Here are two examples at opposite ends of the spectrum:

- A manufacturing firm usually makes a certain component but is too busy in a particular period. It outsources (buys in) the component from another company (often a competitor).

- A university employs groundskeepers. The groundskeepers have secured good wages and working conditions. The university outsources groundskeeping to a private non-union company to save money.

In both these cases, workers and their union might object. In the first case, they might consider these outsourcing activities to be the beginning of a trend that would threaten their jobs. On the one hand, this fear may be entirely unjustified, and the activity may be genuinely one-off to tide the firm over during an exceptional period. The solution here is for workers and management to have open discussions in which the temporary nature of the outsourcing is made clear. Of course, management can outsource, suggesting that it is just temporary, whereas in fact it is the beginning of a process leading to closure. In this case, management are misleading workers in order to prevent unrest and opposition.

In the second case, the interests of the workers and the union are clear. Management might engage in outsourcing in an attempt to reduce the power of unions, focusing on reducing certain operations where the union is strong. This need not be an explicit strategy. Outsourcing can be undertaken simply because the outside suppliers are cheap. However, in cases where suppliers are cheap due to a lack of unions or poor pay and working conditions, unions and working people are weakened.

Outsourcing is also undertaken to achieve numerical flexibility of employment without the expense of layoffs and rehiring. When business is down, employers can cancel orders to the supplying companies, rather than laying off members of their core workforce. This increases job security for employees of the core enterprise. At the same time, it increases insecurity for the employees of the supplying enterprise, who are often unorganised.

In the case of permanent outsourcing, industrial relations will be important in determining the outcome. If, for example, there is little solidarity among workers, no union, high unemployment and ruthless management, then the enterprise will likely contract out and jobs will be lost.

On the other hand, if there is solidarity and a strong union, then management will be reluctant to act unilaterally to close parts of the operation. In these circumstances, management is likely to consider alternatives. Outsourcing can be stopped or even reversed with more operations being brought into the enterprise.

Outsourcing and sub-contracting in all its complexity can occur in both the public and private sectors. Local authorities' provision of bin disposal is an example of a service in relation to which outsourcing has been an issue. There are now examples of outsourcing, sub-contracting and direct provision of this service in Ireland.

In recent research on worker participation undertaken for the Adapt programme, it was found that both management and union members often consider sub-contracting to be inappropriate for discussion under participation. Sub-contracting is very close to outsourcing. Where an enterprise has an order and cannot fulfil if for whatever reason, it may sub-contract another enterprise to produce the order.

Why might workers feel that sub-contracting should not be discussed under participation? While some workers would feel management is more competent to make this kind of decision, it is more likely that workers in this case are "drawing lines". They consider certain things to be so objectionable that they would not accept them under any circumstances.

The issue is not always completely clear-cut. Some strategies of outsourcing can lead to a more efficient specialisation in the core operations of the company. This specialisation and concentration could lead to growth, and can take up the slack created by the closure of the less core parts of the company's activities. This possibility arises from "core competence". Core competence is what an organisation is best at, what its resources — mainly people — are most capable of doing. Many companies have focused on their core competence and made strategic decisions to outsource everything else. Thus a company like Microsoft does not print manuals or press CD-ROMs. It only produces software.

In the context of globalisation, outsourcing is frequently to suppliers in another country. In the clothing industry in Ireland, this has become more and more common. The high labour parts of clothing production are outsourced to operations in countries like Latvia, Morocco and Portugal, where wages are lower. Concentrating in Ireland on design and marketing could result in the company becoming more competitive. But what happens to the jobs of the people in the clothing industry — mainly women — who used to do the sewing? The negative effects of this job loss can cripple entire regions, as has happened in some parts of the United States.

Because the implications of outsourcing are complex, it is important that workers and their union representatives explore the issues and options.

Chapter 17

Marketing the Product

In this chapter:

❖ **What is marketing?**

❖ **Do workers and their unions have a role in marketing?**

The Institute of Marketing defines marketing as:

> *"the management process responsible for identifying, anticipating and satisfying customer requirements profitably"*.

This definition means that people who study marketing actually have a great deal of choice about what to focus on. Marketing goes all the way from basic questions like the best colour for the package to complicated questions like whether and how the enterprise should enter a new market.

The definition appears to focus on the final consumer; that is, the people who buy the final good and eat it, wear it, drive it or whatever. Looked at more closely, it is clear that this is not so. Rather than an individual, the customer could be an enterprise that is going to use the good or service in its own production process. In this case, the supply chain management we described in Chapter 13 becomes a part of marketing.

Do workers and unions have a role in marketing? What has been suggested in most of the discussions in this section of the book is that workers and their unions have a role in everything that the enterprise does.

The best enterprises will probably be the most integrated; that is, all the different functions in the enterprise are planned together. For marketing, this means that it is not considered a completely separate function that comes into play after the product is made. When a new product is being considered, an integrated enterprise might have a multi-skilled, multi-function team involved. There might be a designer, an industrial engineer, a finance person, production employees, and perhaps even people representing the buyer company that will be using the new product. There might also be a marketing representative involved.

In such enterprises — and there are not many — marketing is simply part of the process of producing and supplying the good or service. Workers have no less a role in this than they do in any other part of the production process. Marketing, at its best, in the best companies, is done by everyone who works in the company.

Marketing, at its worst, is the process of conning people into buying something they don't want, that probably is not of the required quality, and that will not be serviced in the future because the company is likely to go out of business.

As with so many of the other elements of business, as we have shown in this section of the book, the role of workers in marketing is two-sided:

- On the one hand, the more the workers see their own futures as related to that of the organisation, the more they will take seriously such things as the public perception of the organisation and its products or services.

- On the other, the more insecure workers feel, the less concerned they are likely to be about the organisation and the way the public sees its products/services.

Chapter 18

Pursuing World Class Manufacturing

In this chapter:

❖ **What is World Class Manufacturing (WCM)?**

❖ **What is the role of workers and their unions in WCM?**

WCM is the pursuit of high performance in quality, lead-time, cost and customer service, through continuous improvement in performance (*Kaizen*), using various other management or organisational philosophies. These may include Just-In-Time (JIT), Total Quality Management (TQM), Total Productive Maintenance (TPM), team-based organisation and employee involvement.

WCM emerged in the 1980s as a way of linking together the various management innovations we have discussed so far. Because WCM is a combination of these other programmes, it contains all the advantages and disadvantages discussed so far for workers and their unions. Very few enterprises can really be considered as having fully implemented WCM.

Why do enterprises move in the direction of WCM? The reasons often relate to the nature of the global economic system and the changes that it has experienced in the last 20 years:

- The massive changes in information, communication and transportation technologies have increased competition.

This demands that companies be more responsive, more quickly, than in the past. If they aren't, their share of the market will decline.

- Enterprises have also been forced to produce goods that are more customised, that is, designed to meet the particular needs of different groups of people, or even individuals.

- The life expectancy of products is much shorter. Whereas in the past a particular model of a car could last for many years, nowadays car manufacturers are being forced to change models every year or two. In the clothing industry, new styles used to be introduced once or twice a year, now changes are much more frequent. In the computer industry, the speed of change is even more rapid. Economists call all this a "shortening of product life cycles".

There are other reasons for change, some of them much more traditional. By introducing new computers and new software frequently, the companies producing these products make the old ones redundant. This has for many years been known as "built-in obsolescence". It was always possible, for example, to produce cars that would last for decades. But car manufacturers that did so would be manufacturing themselves out of the market for new cars. So they built cars that wouldn't last. What some of the advanced electronics companies are doing in their production and marketing strategies is similar. They produce goods knowing that they will be replaced within a year or less by more advanced products.

So one of the factors in enterprises adopting new philosophies is the need to be more flexible, without which they would not be able to respond to the increased competition. But it is also true that under the pressure of increased competition, companies are more likely to pursue any management innovation or fad which promises to improve the bottom line.

Elements of WCM may also be adopted in order to solve specific problems. A manager may aim to reduce inventories through JIT, reduce rejects through TQM, or reduce machine downtime through TPM. This partial, problem-specific adoption of elements of WCM is often a last gasp attempt to survive. A "cherry picking" approach to WCM is one where an attempt is made to introduce only those elements that management considers to be appropriate for its immediate needs. Some experts have argued that such a problem-specific focus is a violation of WCM strategy and that WCM must be adopted as a package.

There are at least ten principles that are common to many of the new forms of work organisation. WCM is like a philosophical umbrella for all these ideas. We have discussed all or most of them already. It should be emphasised that these principles are present together in very few firms, though they are increasing in number.

COMMON PRINCIPLES

1. **Customer orientation.** The "external" or final customer is the source of demand that triggers production.

2. **Teamwork principles.** Who the members are depends on the problem or situation. The team crosses traditional divides to include workers and management in some cases and people from different departments in other cases. Team members may also come from outside the company.

3. **Continuous improvement (Kaizen).** Product, processes and equipment are constantly examined to improve quality, reduce variability and maintain continuity in production.

4. **Total organisational commitment.** Everyone is expected to avoid mistakes. Everyone is expected to improve the way that they do their job. Everyone must be willing to communicate with each other to develop ways to satisfy the customer.

5. **Decisions based on data.** Continuous record-keeping provides the data to be used for team problem-solving.

6. **Simplicity.** Techniques, machines and processes are simple, standardised and documented.

7. **Visibility.** Material flows through workstations are visible. Signals to produce are visual. Relevant information is prominently displayed. (*Kanban* is an example of this.)

8. **Employee "ownership".** This means that line workers are given responsibilities to perform tasks which were traditionally performed by others within the company.

9. **Multi-skilling.** Workers are trained to perform multiple tasks.

10. **Constant training.** Training is needed to develop the skills for effective teamwork. Workers also have to be taught to collect and analyse data. Training is also needed for "multi-skilling".

WORKERS, UNIONS AND WCM

World Class Manufacturing is a broad church. There are many high priests and new scriptures added daily. It is impossible for unions to adopt a single strategy that would fit every instance where WCM is introduced. It is better to adopt some management terminology and assess the *opportunities* and *threats* WCM brings to workers and their unions.

Opportunities

- WCM can provide workers with broader skills and continuous training.

- Workers may be given more latitude to take decisions either by themselves or together with other members of a team.

- Workers and unions can obtain important information about the performance of the enterprise

- Workers and unions can exercise more influence on management decisions and strategy.

- Workers can share in the economic benefits of the improvement in the performance of the enterprise.

Threats

- Unregulated multi-skilling and teamwork can lead to more employer control over work assignments.

- Pressure for continuous improvement can lead to more intensive work and job stress.

- Saved time and effort can lead to fewer jobs.

- Flexibility for the firm can be achieved at the cost of insecurity for the workers.

- Reduction of variance in pursuit of quality can lead to closely controlled and supervised work.

NEW UNION STRATEGIES

Will it be the opportunities or the threats that come to pass? The answer depends on the degree of organisation of workers and how effective they are in pursuing their own interests within the new industrial relations environment. A changing business environment inevitably means unions become more important not less. New developments have to be investigated and understood from the worker's perspective. New strategies have to be formulated and implemented. Now more than ever, workers and their unions must remain alert to the changing scene.

Some new directions for unions have already started to take shape. Today, effective unions:

- Are more proactive than reactive. They must take the initiative in changing various practices in enterprises. They may, for example, initiate a profit sharing or gainsharing scheme, ensuring that workers gain from improvements in the firm's performance in ways that encourage company disclosure and solidarity among workers.

- Undertake research on various topics like new technology. They use their findings, based on the best knowledge and experience available, to advise workers and management on how new technology can be introduced so that it both improves productivity and enhances the jobs and job satisfaction of those using the new technology.

- Aim to secure for their members a say in management. They see union participation in all organisations — private and public sector — as desirable.

- Adopt long-term perspectives, and, in doing so, attempt to offset the tendency of management to focus on short-term profitability. People in satisfying, challenging, well-paid and secure jobs will do their best to ensure that the organisation employing them remains in existence.

> **Today it is important that employees and unions know the rules of the economic game, the basic strategies and how to keep score. We hope this book has helped us move in that direction. Mind your own business!**

Points to take away from Section Three

- ❖ There are many new ways of rewarding workers. It requires careful examination of different systems of pay and rewards to decide which best suits any particular situation.

- ❖ The state and regulation continue to play an important role in the protection of workers' rights.

- ❖ Many new forms of work organisation may either improve or worsen the jobs and rewards of workers, depending on how the changes are introduced.

- ❖ It is not always clear whether a particular change results in working harder or working smarter. In some cases, a change can result in both.

- ❖ Training and skills are extremely important in ensuring job security for individual workers, and, as a result, in maintaining the welfare of the entire community.

- ❖ A successful national system of innovation will contribute to the improvement of a wide range of enterprises in the country.

- ❖ WCM shares the advantages and disadvantages of its various component parts.

- ❖ Unions are reinventing themselves and developing new and more effective strategies in the 21st century.

- ❖ Unions can and do have an important role in the success of organisations pursuing international best practice.

Glossary

Accruals Concept
The accounting principle that profit is the difference between revenues and costs incurred during the period, rather than the difference between actual cash receipts and payments during the period.

Accrued Expenses or **Accruals**
Expenses relating to a period which have not been paid by the end of that period.

Amortisation
The writing off of an asset over a period of time; usually used in relation to intangible assets.

Annualised Hours
An arrangement to match working hours to the operational needs of the enterprise. The annual total of basic working hours is scheduled on a flexible basis. Employees agree to be available to work these and up to a maximum number of additional hours if they are needed. This removes the need for overtime pay. Instead, a higher level of basic pay, based on the value of the total hours, i.e. the basic plus the additional or reserved hours, is paid even if the additional hours are not worked. This provides for flexible working hours and a higher stable basic pay rate.

Approved Profit Sharing Scheme (APSS)

A profit sharing scheme which, in order to obtain certain tax benefits, must be approved by the Revenue Commissioners. Among the criteria for approval is that the scheme be inclusive, and, for example, offer all participating directors and employees participation on the same terms. Among the tax advantages are deductions for setting up and running the scheme, and for the money it diverts into profit sharing.

Assets

Resources of the company which are capable of providing future benefits and which can be measured in monetary terms.

Audit

An independent review of and report on a set of accounts.

Benchmarking

Comparing the performance of a company (for example, in controlling costs or the number of defects) against that of one or more similar companies, or that company itself at a later stage.

Brand

A particular product or group of products, or a characteristic that serves to distinguish a product or products from those of competitors.

Capital Allowances

The amount of depreciation the government decides may be charged in calculating the profit on which tax is payable.

Capitalist Economy

An economy based on private ownership of the means of production and the profit motive. In a capitalist economy, most people must work for wages.

Cellular Manufacturing

The organisation of production in individual cells rather than in long "lines". In the cellular layout, work is physically organised so that a group of machines and/or people complete the product or a number of products. Each cell is a separable and independent part of the production process.

Consumer Price Index (CPI)

This measures changes in the average price of goods and services to consumers. The index reflects 45,000 price checks on 985 common goods and services throughout the country. The index is weighted to reflect the fact that we spend a greater proportion of our incomes on some items than on others.

Creditors

Those to whom a business owes money.

Debenture

Loan to a company formally acknowledged in writing.

Debtors

Those who owe money to a business.

Depreciation

(i) Goods produced which replace used-up stocks and worn-out machinery. (ii) The wearing out, consumption or other reduction in the useful life of an asset arising from use, the passage of time, or obsolescence.

Employee Empowerment

A systematic way of involving employees in improving the organisation and effectiveness of their work. This has also been referred to as Employee Involvement (EI). *Quality Circles* (see below) are a form of employee empowerment.

Employee Share Ownership Plan (ESOP)

A legally established method by which a company distributes shares to its employees, usually linked to profit through an approved profit sharing scheme (APSS).

Financial Period

The period between two balance sheet dates, usually one year.

Fiscal Policy

Involves manipulating the overall demand for goods and services in the economy by adjusting Government spending and/or taxes.

Flexibility

A variety of ways in which rapid rates of change in organisations can be facilitated, including functional, numerical, operational and wage flexibility. They all involve greater freedom for management

— sometimes with appropriate compensation for employees — to respond rapidly to changing market or technological conditions.

Gainsharing
An incentive system that rewards employees for improved performance. The amount of gain is calculated using a previously agreed formula and shared between employees and the company.

GDP
Short for Gross Domestic Product. The money value of all the goods and services produced for the market in the year.

GNP
Short for Gross National Product. Similar to GDP except that net payments overseas are subtracted out.

Government Deficit
The part of government expenditure that exceeds government income.

Group Undertaking
Any company which is part of the same group of companies as the company whose financial statements are being considered ("the reporting company"). For example, if the reporting company is a subsidiary, then its parent is a group undertaking, as is any other subsidiary company of the same parent; if the reporting company is a parent, then its subsidiary is a group undertaking.

Inflation Rate
An increase in the overall price level.

Just-in-Time (JIT)
The organisation of supply of inputs, of production, and of delivery of finished products, so as to reduce or remove the need for inventory or buffer stocks of parts. (See also Kanban.)

Kaizen
A Japanese word meaning continuous process improvement. This usually involves measuring what people do (in either a manufacturing or service sector environment) and providing incentives for them to work together, often in quality circles, to improve productivity and product or service quality.

Kanban
A Japanese word meaning "card", this is one type of JIT system in which cards are used as signals to pull parts into production when they are required.

Liabilities
Financial obligations of a business, frequently money owed.

Limited Company
A company in which the obligation of shareholders to contribute to its liabilities is limited to the amounts that they have already paid for their shares and any amounts which may be outstanding on partly paid-for shares. The shareholders' exposure to the company's debts is limited.

Matching Concept
The accounting principle that in computing profit, costs or expenses should be matched against the revenues which they helped create.

Monetary Policy
Involves maniputlating the overall demand for goods and services in the economy through interest rate changes.

Multi-skilling
This makes firms more flexible by giving employees the opportunities, skills and training to master a wider repertoire of challenging jobs. This should not be confused with "multi-tasking", which simply involves shifting workers between routine tasks as required by operational pressures.

National Debt
Money the government owes as a result of past government deficits.

National System of Innovation
The formal state and company organisations that encourage innovation, together with the more informal educational, cultural, and institutional factors that interact to make a society innovative.

Net Product
Total product minus the depreciation.

Partnership

A process of co-operative relations between an employer and a union. This is based on the establishment of joint employer–union aims for the enterprise, the involvement of union representatives and employees in strategic and operational decision-making and the sharing of the financial gains (profits or savings) that accrue to the enterprise.

Patent

Exclusive right to the use of an invention.

PEPPER Schemes

Schemes that provide for **P**articipation by **E**mployed **P**ersons in **P**rofits and **E**nterprise **R**esults. They can be based on profit sharing or employee share ownership.

Profit Margin

The profit before interest and taxation as a percentage of sales.

Profit Sharing

An arrangement whereby employees receive some portion of a company's profit. To obtain tax incentives, profit sharing schemes must be approved by the Revenue Commissioners, i.e. they must be APSS, or approved profit sharing schemes.

Prudence Concept

The accounting principle that accountants should err on the side of caution in recognition of revenue and expenses.

Quality Circles

A type of team, developed in Japan, focusing on the improvement of quality. It is usually made up of between five and ten people, often from different levels in the organisation, who meet regularly to discuss quality-related work problems and suggest — and eventually implement — solutions.

Revenue

The gross income of a company.

Social Benchmarking

The identification and measurement of factors that affect the experience of working in an enterprise. While process benchmarking deals with enterprise operational effectiveness (see *Benchmarking* above) social benchmarking measures the employees' experiences of morale, motivation, equality, participation etc. Social benchmarking can be used to improve the employees' experience of working in the enterprise.

Standards
The costs allowed by a company's management for each element (such as materials and labour) in the manufacture of the company's products.

Statistical Process Control (SPC)
A data-based quality control system, the aim of which is to monitor the variation in each operation's output, leading to changes in processes so as to reduce the variation (and related wastage).

Surplus Product
What's left from the total product after the depreciation and the wage goods are taken out. The source of profits produced by labour.

Taylorism (or Scientific Management)
Control by management of what happens on the shop floor through detailed knowledge obtained, for example, by studying the movements of workers and then subdividing the work into component parts. These can then be monitored through time and motion studies.

Teams
An occupational unit or group with from five to 20 members who have a range of complementary skills and who work together on a common task for which they each have equal responsibility.

Total Preventive Maintenance (TPM)
The prevention of breakdowns in equipment through the transfer of maintenance jobs, where appropriate, to machine operators.

Total Product
All the goods and services produced in a year.

Total Quality Management (TQM)
Involves the commitment to prevent all defects by everyone involved in production of a good or provision of a service, so as to ensure conformance to specifications.

Trademark

A distinctive identification of a product or service, the exclusive use of which is protected by law.

Turnover

The sales of a company arising through the provision of products or services to its customers.

Wage Goods

All goods and services consumed by working people. The standard of living of the working class.

Worker Participation

The representative participation by employees in the management of the enterprise. Sometimes interchanged with "industrial democracy". Elected worker directors and union/worker representatives on below-board management structures are key elements in worker participation along with the disclosure to workers and their union representatives of company financial and business information.

World Class Manufacturing (WCM)

The pursuit of superior performance in quality, lead-time, cost and customer service through continuous improvement in performance (Kaizen), using various other new forms of work organisation like JIT, TQM and TPM.

Index